"Packed with practical and easy-to-understand advice from someone who's been there, *The Debt Escape Plan* is a must-read for anyone who faces the challenging goal of getting out of credit card debt. Harzog's perfect blend of empathy, sound advice and humor will keep you motivated until you're debt-free."
—Farnoosh Torabi, financial expert and award-winning author of *When She Makes More*

"Beverly Harzog has personally experienced the pain and stress of credit card debt. This insightful book will help everyone who is trying to dig out of debt and rebuild their financial life."
—Bill Hardekopf, CEO of LowCards.com

"When it comes to getting out of debt, Beverly Harzog knows what she's talking about. Not only is she a leading expert on credit and financial issues, she's been there herself and understands the difficult decisions you face."
—Gerri Detweiler, Talk Credit Radio host and Director of Consumer Education at Credit.com

"Americans are drowning in debt. And with a boatload of debt comes bad credit. In her new book, *The Debt Estate Plan*, Beverly Harzog provides excellent advice to help American families pay down their debts, clean up their credit and live a financially easier life. Everyone will benefit from this terrific information."
—Ilyce Glink, Award-winning personal finance writer and publisher, ThinkGlink.com

"Beverly's first book *Confessions of a Credit Junkie* was chock full of personal experiences and sound advice for people who have gotten in over their heads with debt. In *The Debt Escape Plan*, she goes into great detail about how to get rid of the problem—forever."

—Steve Ely, CEO of eCredable.com

THE
DEBT
ESCAPE
PLAN

How to Free Yourself From Credit Card Balances,
Boost Your Credit Score, and Live Debt-Free

BEVERLY HARZOG

CAREER
PRESS

This edition first published in 2015 by Career Press, an imprint of
Red Wheel/Weiser, LLC
With offices at:
65 Parker Street, Suite 7
Newburyport, MA 01950
www.redwheelweiser.com
www.careerpress.com

ISBN: 978-1-60163-360-6
Library of Congress Cataloging-in-Publication Data
Harzog, Beverly Blair.
  The debt escape plan : how to free yourself from credit card balances,
boost your credit score, and live debt-free / by Beverly Harzog.
      pages cm
  Includes index.
  ISBN 978-1-60163-360-6 -- ISBN 978-1-60163-392-7 (ebook) 1.
Finance, Personal. 2. Consumer credit. 3. Debt. I. Title.

  HG179.H3188 2015
  332.024'02--dc23
                                                        2014045679

Cover design by Rob Johnson/Toprotype
Interior by Gina Schenck

Printed in the United States of America
IBI
10 9 8 7 6 5 4 3 2 1

This book is dedicated to everyone who is working hard to get out of credit card debt. Don't give up—you can do it!

Acknowledgments

I'm incredibly lucky when it comes to family. I spent the summer of 2014 writing this book. I wrote during our beach vacation and no one complained. I also wrote a book during the summer of 2013, so they certainly had a right to be tired of my constant deadlines. But they stood by me and supported me with love and patience. Thank you Bernd, Ashley, and Grant for always being there for me. I'm so blessed to have such a loving and giving family.

I owe a world of gratitude to my agent, Marilyn Allen. We've now done three books together. Marilyn, thank you for believing in me and in my ideas. You're not just my agent; you're a great friend, and I'm so glad I get to work with you. You're the best agent ever!

One of the reasons I wrote this book is because I got so many e-mails from my readers who want tips on how to get out of credit card debt. So a big thanks to all of you who have reached out to me, because *you* inspired this book. My hope is that this book will help you get out of—and stay out of—debt. Thank you for putting your trust in me!

I also want to thank the awesome folks at Career Press. I feel lucky to have a publisher that produces such great work. Thank you to Michael Pye, Adam Schwartz, and Kirsten Dalley for being a joy to work with and for doing such a great job on my books. And special thanks to Gerri Detweiler for being so generous with her advice and for being such a great friend.

When it comes to friendships, I struck gold. For months, I had friends cheering me on. Those same friends also listened when I was tired and cranky from all the writing. So I want to give a special thanks to Rosie Russell, Mary Ann Campbell, Kerri Fivecoat-Campbell, Linda Melone, Michele Wojciechowski, and Karen Cordaway for your emotional support and friendship. You ladies rock!

Contents

Introduction

When I was in my 20s, I managed to rack up more than $20,000 in credit card debt. I have no excuse for my situation. I spent a ridiculous amount of my time shopping and I never tracked my spending. It didn't take long for me to start carrying balances on my credit cards from month to month. I should have been alarmed the first time this happened, but I didn't even bat an eye. Carrying a balance become my new normal.

Before long, I was maxed out on seven different credit cards. Seven! My shopping addiction had an emotional element, for sure. I focused on expensive clothes and designer shoes. All of these things were supposed to give me more confidence at work. It actually did—for about one day. Like a drug, the high eventually wore off; it was all an illusion. Confidence comes from within, not from wearing an Armani suit or carrying a Gucci handbag.

Once the thrill of a new outfit wore off, I'd have to go shopping again to get back the high and the temporary confidence boost. The cycle continued to repeat itself until I had my "rock bottom" moment when my favorite credit card was canceled. At that point, I decided it was time to take back my life, and I devised a debt escape plan for myself. With my plan, I paid off more than $20,000 in credit card debt in two years. Granted, I didn't have kids at the time, but I still think two years is pretty darn good.

After my previous book, *Confessions of a Credit Junkie*, was published, I received a lot of e-mails from readers who told me that they loved my book, but wish they'd read it before they got into credit card debt. I received so many of these e-mails that I decided I needed to write a book about getting out of credit card debt. There are a lot of books out there about debt. Many of them are written by well-known experts whom I admire. But clearly, people were still looking for a solution to their debt dilemma. So I decided it was time to offer another solution.

I spent about six months just researching credit card debt and the books that were already on the market. I didn't want to produce a book that just mirrored what was already available. You know what else I did? I reread all the e-mails I'd received from my awesome readers. I read all the Amazon reviews that were written about dozens and dozens of debt-related books. I thought carefully about the steps I took when I decided to get out of debt.

When I looked at all the information and research, two things stood out. Most debt books focus on too much at once—every debt you have—or recommend a one-size-fits-all strategy. There are many different types of debt. Student loans, mortgages, car loans, personal loans, and more. It doesn't make sense to use the same strategy on different types of debt, and it really and truly doesn't make sense to assume that every person can use one standard approach to get out of debt. We're all different, and we all have a unique way of interacting with the world. So while the one-size-fits-all approach seems to work for some, there are others who just get left behind in the dust. It's like trying to put a square peg in a round hole: It doesn't work because it's not a good fit.

So this book focuses exclusively on credit card debt. It also takes a unique approach. You'll take the Money Personality Quiz in Chapter 3. This will help you figure out which debt-elimination strategy will work best for you given your money type and your learning style. Trust me, it will be fun!

Best of all, you won't be pressured into using a strategy that doesn't work for you. You'll receive guidance on how to choose a budgeting method and a debt strategy, but the choice will be yours. *The Debt Escape Plan* will show you how to pay off your credit cards and boost your credit score. You'll also learn how to live debt-free so you never, ever get into credit card debt again.

Are you ready to break the chains of debt and take back your life? Let's do this!

1

9 Mistakes That Keep
You Stuck in Debt

Being in debt is a horrible feeling, isn't it? Anyone who has ever been in debt knows that. I've been there to the tune of $20,000, so I really can empathize. But you know what's even worse than feeling like you're about to go under water? Making mistakes that cause you to sink even *lower* into the depths of debt hell.

I've actually committed *all* of the mistakes I'm going to cover here. Yep, all nine! It's not an achievement I'm particularly proud of, but by sharing it with you I'm hoping you'll benefit from my past misery. Some of these mistakes I made just as I was starting to sink into debt. They're what I like to call "gateway mistakes"; once you get comfortable with these mistakes, you're just a few steps away from the bigger mistakes that take you all the way down the rabbit hole.

So, I know firsthand how screwed up things can get. I also know that these nine mistakes kept me in debt far longer than necessary. And that means I paid a whole lot more in interest than I would have if I'd come to my senses sooner. Here's the deal: Face these mistakes head-on so you can nip them in the bud and get on with fixing your life. Of course, if you're afflicted with Mistake #1, I know that this is easier said than done.

Mistake #1: You Have an Acute Case of Head-in-Sand Syndrome

When you're in debt, you kind of wish you could have a do-over with your credit cards. This is especially true if you've taken the time to learn about your finances since you got into debt. If you could climb into a time machine and go back a few years, you definitely would not buy those designer shoes. And you wouldn't even think about getting that awesome flat-screen TV again. In fact, if you could bargain with the shopping gods, you'd never buy anything again, ever!

If you could only erase the damage, you'd be the best cardholder who has ever lived. See, this is the kind of thinking that leads to depression, because you know you can't have a do-over with your credit card debt. And this, my friends, is what makes you vulnerable to head-in-sand syndrome (HISS).

Here are some of the unpleasant side effects of HISS: When you're in the acute stage, you might start making late payments. Or worse, you might even stop paying your bills altogether, as I did. Other side effects include plunging credit scores, mail-induced nausea, and non-existent self-esteem. It's not surprising that some of us start to pretend that the whole debt thing doesn't even exist. I mastered this approach when I was in debt. Fortunately, this syndrome is curable by taking a large dose of reality. I call this "staring down your debt," and I show you exactly how to do just that in Chapter 2.

When I was in debt I had seven credit cards, and they were all maxed out. Every. Single. One. You know what happens when you're in this situation? You get lots and lots of bills in the mail. Yes, I mean snail mail. It was the '80s, and if you could breathe, you could get a credit card. And these were the days before the Internet and digital statements. If you're under the age of 35, this situation is probably difficult to imagine.

My problem wasn't just the amount of debt, though. I had so many high minimum monthly payments, I couldn't pay all of my monthly bills. The electricity, my rent, you name it. Not happening. Fortunately my car was paid for, or I surely would have ended up walking to work. It became overwhelming, and honestly, I wasn't yet ready to face what I'd done. So I made what I considered a logical decision at the time: I stopped going to my mailbox. No mail, no bills, no stress. Problem solved!

I talk about this a bit in my book *Confessions of a Credit Junkie*, and how I went on like this for weeks. But one day I was ambushed by the postal carrier who could no longer stuff any more mail into my mailbox. He happened to be there when I went home for lunch one day, and he said he thought I'd moved and had neglected to fill out one of those mail-forwarding forms. I fibbed about losing my mailbox key and he promptly handed me all my mail. That day, my lovely imaginary life got a jolt of reality.

Unfortunately, during my break from reality, everything had deteriorated to the point of ugliness. Some of my accounts had gone to collection agencies. My electricity was about to be turned off. Serious stuff was happening because I refused to live in reality. Would you believe I continued on in this semi-comatose state just a bit longer? When you feel like the walls are closing in on you, you cope the best way you can while you try to figure out what to do next. It might look to outsiders like you're making insane decisions. But this is why I never, ever judge the decisions people make when they're in debt. It's kind of like floating in the ocean, hanging onto a life preserver during a big storm. You're just trying to keep your head above water while you wait for things to calm down.

But the only way to keep from drowning is to face reality. Trust me on this. When I finally came to my senses, I had a strangely Zen type of feeling. I think I was relieved that the credit ride was over. Now, I just had to figure out how to take back my life.

Of course, I regretted not having this epiphany sooner. My head-in-sand time made things worse than they already were, which made my credit comeback more difficult. But I still managed to recover from this mistake, and you can, too.

Mistake #2: You Believe You're a Victim

This one is complicated. I want to be sensitive here because there really are unfortunate circumstances, such as a health crisis or sudden unemployment, that make it difficult for people to pay their bills. In these cases, I'm not criticizing you for feeling like you've been dealt a bad hand. But until you can stop identifying yourself as the victim, you won't be able to pay off your debt. You'll be too angry to stay focused, because getting out of debt isn't for the faint of heart; it's hard work, and you have to be all in.

Let's take a look at the two most common complaints I hear from those who get stuck in victim roles. We'll take a look at each scenario and I'll explain what I mean.

"The credit card companies tricked me."

Some personal finance experts will tell you it isn't your fault. You couldn't resist the advertisements. They were too powerful, and you got sucked into buying stuff. Well, I'm not one of those experts. I happen to think that you're smarter than that and not weak-minded enough to get continually sucked into purchases you don't need. Sure, we all indulge in impulse buys now and then, but you can't blame $30,000 of credit card debt on commercials or complicated fine print.

I have a lot of respect for you. I think you're tough and savvy. And I think that deep down inside, you know that. Am I right? So let me give it to you straight: *It's your debt and you're responsible for paying it off.* It's really that simple. I don't want to hear that you bought into the hype or the advertisements made you do it. It doesn't matter how funny the credit card commercial was; it was still your responsibility to read the fine print. And yes, I agree some of the fine print is deceptive and tricky. But at some point, it was up to you to stop the spending.

Now, there are other circumstances that don't involve impulse buys or being influenced by ads. Let's take a look at these because, really, I understand why these situations would make you feel mad at the world. In fact, you wouldn't be normal if you weren't feeling a little victimized.

"I experienced a crisis."

Losing your job, going through a messy divorce, and being diagnosed with a life-threatening illness all fall into this category. These are situations that often cause a lot of folks to sink into debt. If you're a parent, this is even more complex because you have mouths to feed. You can't decide to eat canned tuna fish (or my personal favorite, peanut butter and jelly sandwiches) for six months while you try to fix your money situation. Kids need a good diet, and they grow quickly. When my kids were young, it seemed like they needed new shoes every three months.

So let me just say that I really do feel badly for you. This is a debt situation that isn't fair. I get that. Maybe you even had an emergency fund, but it wasn't enough to survive the long months without a steady income or out-of-pocket medical expenses you had to cover. But here's the harsh reality: *It's still your debt and you have to pay it off.* Find a way to re-create yourself as a survivor. You faced tough times and you survived. Now you've got credit card debt, but you'll beat that, too.

If you're in debt due to an illness or a family member's illness, this has become, unfortunately, an all-too-common financial crisis. The number-one cause of bankruptcy in this country is medical debt. You might be in a situation where you have such high medical bills, you see no way out. And if you're way over your head in medical debt, I address this specific situation in Chapter 8.

Mistake #3: You Fail to Identify the Real Problem

This is a common mistake and I know why. It takes a bit of work and soul searching to sort this out. And I'm talking about narrowing down your problem to the *exact* source. So saying "I spend too much time at the mall" isn't specific enough. If you don't isolate the specific source of your problem, you can't make the necessary adjustments. And even if you manage to get out of debt, you're likely to end up in debt again. I'll cover this in more detail in Chapter 2, but I want you to start giving this some thought now. So let's look at a few of the more common reasons people end up in credit card debt.

Retail therapy

This type of behavior goes by many names: shopaholic, mall rat, or—my personal favorite—credit junkie. The incentive is the same, though. You experienced a disappointment, got upsetting news, broke a nail, rear-ended another car, had a boring afternoon. Just insert the verb/crummy adjective/noun combo that applies to you.

Remember the experiment with Pavlov's dogs? Ivan Pavlov did an experiment that conditioned dogs to salivate when they heard a bell. When they heard the bell, they knew they'd soon be getting meat powder. This is called classical conditioning. I'm not suggesting we're exactly like Pavlov's dogs (although I've been called worse things on the Internet!), but the theory still applies.

This is what happens: A certain trigger in your life compels you to react with your credit card. Then you go shopping and it gives you a psychological boost just when you need it. When I was in debt, I specialized in head-in-sand syndrome and retail therapy. Had a bad day at the office? A new pair of Ralph Lauren jeans sounded about right. Broke up with a boyfriend? The therapy required depended on how much I liked him. If I thought he was The One, designer shoes were sure to kill the pain. Oddly enough, I needed more therapy to recover from the jerks. I once bought a luxurious winter coat after a breakup with a guy I was actually glad to get rid of.

The truth is, we all engage in retail therapy now and then. An Ebates.com survey in 2013 showed that 51.8 percent of Americans shop and spend a little now and then when they need to feel better. Women, at 63 percent, did this quite a bit more than men, at 39 percent. So a little retail therapy on occasion isn't the issue. But if you indulge in retail therapy on a frequent basis, it's really difficult to get out of debt because you're still busy getting *into* debt. You have to put down the credit cards. You'll need a new way to handle the ups and downs of life.

You know what worked for me? I learned everything I could about personal finance, especially credit. I know that sounds painfully dull, but it was so empowering. And well, I admit that I kind of like feeling powerful. It raised my self-esteem and self-confidence to levels I'd never had before.

Ironically, confidence issues turned out to be my spending catalyst. It wasn't that I needed to shop to forget my bad day at the office. *Every* day was a bad day at the office. I had a bad day because I wasn't advancing in my career the way I wanted to. The cause? Poor self-confidence. I needed new shoes to regain my confidence. So when I walked into the office the next day, it was a whole new me. And I loved the compliments about how great I looked. But as soon as the newness wore off, I was right back where I started.

When I'm on the radio, I'm often asked if I got credit counseling to overcome my credit junkie tendencies. I never saw a credit counselor about this because once I decided to pay off my debt, I became more self-disciplined. I also didn't know that credit counseling was out there and that it was a good option if I wanted to pursue it.

Just watching my debt total go down generated an adrenaline response that was similar to the rush I once got when I scored a new handbag at the mall. There was a big emotional component to my spending, for sure. I do feel lucky that learning about personal finance boosted my confidence and self-esteem enough to help me control my spending.

If you've tried to stop shopping and you can't, there's no shame in that. We all have something that, at one time, has held us back from getting what we wanted. If you think counseling would help, then don't hesitate to try it. Many counselors will work on a sliding scale and only charge you what you can pay. I realize this is not the best way to immediately pay down debt since it involves spending more money. But we're thinking about long-term solutions here. It always pays off to spend time working on yourself, if that helps you succeed in getting rid of your debt.

Now, if you feel your shopping has approached the level of addiction, I urge you to contact Debtors Anonymous for help. I have contact information for you in Appendix B. Do whatever you need to do to take back your life. It's no one else's business how you going about doing this.

Spending too much time with shopaholic friends

Anytime you're trying to give up something, you likely need to keep away from the thing you're trying to give up. If most of your friends think browsing and shopping at the mall is the way to spend a Saturday, then you need to cut back on the time you spend with them. Now, this assumes that they would pressure you into buying something. But let's be honest: It's hard to pass over a dress that's just the right size and in a color that brings out your eyes unless you're in a good place psychologically.

I know it's difficult to cut back on your time with friends, and they may not understand at first. But I think you need to be honest. I really believe that's the best way to save a friendship. Let them know that you're working on getting out of debt. If you don't want to talk about that, then tell them you're saving money for something you really want. That's true, too. You're saving money to throw at your debt because you want it to go away!

This is a complex problem, and I know you don't want to give up your friends—unless, of course, they are sabotaging your efforts to get out of debt. You know that saying "misery loves company"? Well, that's how we sometimes end up with friends who aren't good for our emotional and financial health. Only you can decide if you need new friends. All I'm saying is that you need to take a look at who you hang out with while you're in the midst of debt reduction.

Mistake #4: You Don't Make Credit Card Debt Your Priority

We've already talked about how quickly the interest can pile up. We'll talk about different approaches to paying off your credit cards later in the book. But the main thing to get into your head right now is that you can't put it off. You can't decide to save for a new car before paying off your credit cards. And definitely don't pay off your mortgage before you pay off credit card debt.

You've probably heard of the concept of good debt vs. bad debt. Good debt is associated with an investment— a mortgage, for example. This assumes you make a good choice and don't overpay for a home. Although it isn't the clear-cut financial win it used to be, most of us still want to own a home. It's a source of pride and often brings a tax deduction. This all assumes you don't get a mortgage you can't really afford, of course.

Student loans are another example of good debt. You're making an investment in your future. A recent Pew Research Center study showed that Millennials aged 25 to 32 who had college degrees earned a median salary of $45,500, whereas high school graduates earned only $28,000 (from "The Rising Cost of Not Going to College," Pew Research Social and Demographic Trends, February 11, 2014, *www.pewsocialtrends.org/2014/02/11/the-rising-cost-of-not-going-to-college/#*). That's a big gap. And the unemployment rate for high-school grads was three times higher than it was for those with a college degree. But if you go overboard with student loans, you might not gain the advantage you seek. A good rule of thumb is that your student loans should not exceed the amount you expect to make in your first year of work. Another example is a business loan. It's risky, for sure, but your plan is to use the capital you borrow to create a business that provides a source of income. This is what I mean by good debt. You take a calculated risk when you borrow, but you gain something that could make you better off financially down the road.

Okay, now let's take a look at bad debt. With bad debt, you're borrowing money for something that won't appreciate in value. In fact, it might cost you more money than you ever dreamed possible. For example, credit card debt is bad debt. *Very* bad debt. You pay interest on your balances and often end up paying a lot more for your purchases than you ever intended to. There's no anticipation that your new leather boots will appreciate, right? And you know that fancy Mac computer you just bought will be outdated in a year (well, the way technology progresses, maybe less than a year).

Another bad debt is a car loan. Every year, your car decreases in value. If you have an accident, then you lose value even more quickly. I don't buy new cars. Not ever. I do buy cars that are known for lasting a long time, but I buy them when they're a few years old. My last "new" car was seven years old when I bought it, but it only had 57,000 miles on it. My husband does a great job tracking down these jewels. I admit I don't have the patience to do it myself.

Now, if you're a person who enjoys a fine car, that's fine. We all have certain luxuries we enjoy. Just be aware that an auto loan is bad debt. If you must get an expensive car, make sure you don't have any other bad debt at the same time.

So the point is this: If you have bad debt, like credit card debt, *don't shove it into the background while you focus on what you consider to be more important debt.* Make your mortgage payment and your student loan payment on time, of course. But throw your extra money at the bad debt first.

Mistake #5: You Only Make Minimum Payments on Your Credit Card Balances

This is a biggie, folks. If you're barely keeping your head above water, you're excused from this rant. If just reading this makes you feel overwhelmed or angry, I suggest you take a look at Chapter 8. That chapter will help you decide if you can get out of debt on your own or if you need to consider other options.

This mistake and my suggestions to fix it pertain to those who have the money to make bigger payments but aren't making the effort. It might be because you don't clearly understand the impact of compound interest and how much money you're wasting every year. Or you've got a mild case of head-in-sand syndrome so you're making payments on time to keep your score afloat. But other than that, you don't want to think about strategy or the mess you're in. In Chapter 4 and Chapter 5, I'll show you how to find "extra" money in your budget so you can end your debt misery as soon as possible. But for those who think I'm overstating the impact of compound interest, here's an example so you understand what I mean.

Let's assume you have $10,000 in credit card debt. And to make it easy for yours truly, let's say it's on one credit card and the APR (annualized percentage rate) is 15%. I used the calculator provided on the Bankrate.com Website because, well, I'm not a computer. And I like their financial tools.

Now, minimum payment calculations vary a little by issuer, but we'll assume this method to make it easy: interest plus 1% of balance.

In this example, your minimum payment for the first month is $225. If you only make the minimum required payment every month, it will take you 335 months—that's 27.9 years!—to pay off your debt. During these 27.9 years, you will have paid $11,979.29 in interest. Wow, right? You'll end up paying more in interest expense than your original debt total. That's crazy!

Let's take a more aggressive approach to debt repayment. Now, you double the initial $225 minimum payment to $450. The results: Now you pay off your debt in 27 months, or two years and three months. You pay $1,788.72 in interest. Quite a difference! Not just in the amount of interest paid, but in the length of time you stay in debt. Do you want to pay off your debt in two years, as I did? Increase your payment to $500. The result: You're debt-free in 24 months! You pay a total of $1,579.47 in interest.

Okay, so now you see the power of compound interest and how to disarm it with an increase in your monthly payments. Yes, I know that many of you can't find the money in your budget to use this strategy. But some of you can and should take this approach. As I mentioned before, we'll cover this in detail when you create your own debt escape plan. This is why one generalized debt-reduction plan doesn't work for everyone. We all have different cash flows, responsibilities, and credit scores. And we all have different personalities and organizational skills.

Mistake #6: You Try to Keep Up With the Joneses

You know what? I almost didn't include this because I find it hard to believe anyone would buy a Mercedes because there's one in the driveway next door. But the more I thought about it, I realized that, these days, it's not just about keeping up with the Joneses next door; it's also about keeping up with the virtual Joneses online. It really is a complicated and visually driven world we live in today.

Social media, especially Facebook, has created a sort of virtual competition among users. The Facebook Joneses often share photos of fabulous vacations to Italy and their new sports cars. They have successful careers and they never have a bad day at work. Or a bad hair day. Their children are honor students, star athletes, or president of the student council. Or all three!

I remember being at a holiday party a few years ago. A woman was complaining about her teenaged daughter's $400-plus Coach handbag being stolen from her high school locker. Seriously? I don't think I've spent that much on handbags in my entire life. And we're talking decades' worth of handbags. This is an example of a parent trying to keep up with the Joneses kids, which is a horrible attitude to pass down to your kids. I wanted to make like Cher in *Moonstruck*, and slap her and yell, "Snap out it!"

Think of the Facebook Joneses as the virtual version of the annoying Christmas letter you get from that friend or relative who appears to have a perfect life. Maybe half of the letter isn't even true, but it's still enough to get you to question your life and compare it to someone else's who seems to have more money than you. The keyword here is "seems." Honestly, there's a good chance that the Joneses, either the real version or the Facebook version, are in debt up to their eyeballs. That's the part you don't see. Whether it's your neighbors, a Facebook friend, or the annoying Christmas letter person, you have no clue if they can actually afford to live this way. This might be an issue of conspicuous consumption, which is a term that refers to consumers who buy expensive things for the sole purpose of showing others how wealthy they are.

But there are other subtle ways we keep up with the Joneses that aren't usually talked about. Your office can be a breeding ground for competitive behavior, and this extends to material possessions that have little to do with where you work. I was a little bit different in this regard. When I was buying designer clothes it wasn't to keep up with others in the office. On many days, I was the best-dressed person there. That was my problem! I spent the money to boost how I felt about myself. It had nothing to do with what anyone else was wearing. In fact, I rarely noticed what other people wore. It really was, in fact, all about me. However, I can recall how important the car and house discussions were at some of my other jobs. It was important to have a great car and a nice house.

I think these kind of conversations about what we own does create some pressure to measure up. Unemployment has been high for a long time, and many if not most of us feel a little anxious about doing well at our jobs. Jobs aren't easily replaced. If you work in an office where everyone dresses nicely, you'll feel like you need to dress nicely, too. That's just survival at its most basic level. You will have problems getting ahead at work if you don't look like you fit in with the culture. But, if you take it a step further and decide you need to wear a more expensive suit than the man or woman in the office next to you, you're spending more than you need to. At this point, you are not only keeping up with them; you're competing with and trying to one-up them.

Maybe finding out that the Joneses are leveraged up the wazoo won't change your behavior. But do think about how stressed you are buying things to keep up. Really, when it comes time to pay the bills, is it worth it to be in debt? Stop worrying about what others think and live your life debt-free. You'll not only be happier than the Joneses, but you'll also have an emergency account and a retirement fund. In closing, keep this thought in mind:

> *Never keep up with the Joneses: drag*
> *them down to your level. It's cheaper.*

—Quentin Crisp, *The Naked Civil Servant*

Mistake #7: You Think Personal Finance Is for Nerds

Seriously, you're out of high school. Give up the ghost of wedgies past. No one is going to keep you from sitting at the cool table at your local Chili's restaurant just because you know your credit-utilization ratio. (By the way, your credit-utilization ratio is the amount of credit used compared to the amount of credit you have available. More on that later.)

Remember I said I felt empowered when I learned about money management? It's like learning any new skill. If you stick with it and practice what you learn, you'll master it. Mastery builds confidence and self-esteem. Heck, I'll come right out and say it: Fiscal mastery is sexy!

In 2012, the *New York Times* did a small survey and asked how important credit scores were when considering dating someone. Many responders said that having a good credit score was a prerequisite for a date. There are even dating sites that focus on credit scores. I think there's a trend to think about these issues because it can impact your ability to buy things as a couple, such as a house.

Whenever I hear someone say that personal finance is boring and they can't be bothered, I know I'm talking to someone who's mired in Mistake #7. When I was in debt, I devoured books and magazines on this topic. The Internet wasn't invented yet, or I would have used that resource to my advantage, too. These days it's so easy just to hop online and pick a personal finance Website that has tons of information. You can even pick sites that cater to your specific needs. My Website features credit card reviews that I do on request. I spend a lot of time reviewing secured credit cards, in particular, because I noticed that no one was reviewing them in painstaking detail the way I do. I have no affiliate relationships with credit card issuers so you can trust that my reviews are unbiased.

I also write posts from a consumer advocate's point of view about how to benefit from credit cards, how to boost credit scores, and how to get out of credit card debt. So embrace your inner nerd and become a master of personal finance. If you need to learn credit card basics so you can use credit cards more responsibly, check out my book *Confessions of a Credit Junkie*. You'll learn everything you need to know about the basics of using credit cards as well as how to profit from them. Your geek credentials will be complete.

Mistake #8: You Don't Know You Can Ask for Help

No matter how bad your situation is, there are a few steps you can take to help yourself. I'll bet you didn't know that credit card companies have hardship departments. It isn't publicized because it's there for those who really, really need the help and who have a really, really good reason for being in debt.

Hardship departments at credit card companies

I hate to have to say this, but I'll bet you probably believe it, too: There are people out there who will lie to get out of paying a debt simply because they don't want to. They'd really rather not have to pay for their purchases. But I know that you want to do the right thing and pay it off. You just need help to get there. I respect that and I encourage you to pursue every option that offers relief.

I've talked about how some folks get into debt because they've experienced something terrible in their lives, such as unemployment, divorce, or a serious illness. Hardship programs are designed to help cardholders who are in these predicaments. What can you expect in terms of relief? It will vary, of course, but the possibilities include a lower interest rate, lower minimum payments, and/or waived fees.

If you think your account is about to be sent to collections, this strategy may be an option. Just know that the program can last anywhere from six months to a year, and you have to be very diligent and pay as agreed or you could be dropped from the program.

I'm not going to encourage you to use this kind of program if you got into debt the way I did—that is, you went to the mall or the electronics mega-store and bought whatever you wanted without thinking about the financial obligation. Six months later you finally looked at your balance and wondered how the heck it all happened!

If this scenario applies to you, and you call the issuer and tell them how you really got into debt, it might actually make things worse. For example, I know a successful professional who makes a lot of money (well into six figures) but was deep in debt. He called the issuer and told a tale of overspending that was based on "wants" rather than "needs." I admire this person's honesty, but sometimes you just need to keep your mouth shut.

I wasn't surprised to hear that the credit card company had a different take on it. They lowered his credit limit because he scared the daylights out of them. It looked like he didn't understand the value of money. The lower credit limit made his utilization ratio go up; as a result, his credit score dropped even more. Again, while I admire his honesty, sometimes it pays to keep your mouth shut. This is a guy who's successful in his field and expected to get what he was asking for due to his status in life. But it doesn't always work that way.

Credit card debt is an equal-opportunity problem. Here's the possible profile of someone in debt: male, female, low income, high income, middle class, PhD, high-school grad, high-school dropout, has a master's degree, dentist, home owner, apartment dweller, owns a lake house, CPA, carpenter, lawyer, plumber, and on and on. *Anyone* can end up in debt.

And just one more thing before we move on. Please, for the love of God, don't call and lie to the hardship department. These programs are designed for consumers who have suffered some awful personal circumstances. If it gets abused, these programs won't be able to help those who really need it. Lying to gain an advantage could also put you in a precarious position legally and financially.

I'll give the nitty-gritty details on hardship departments when you're designing your own debt escape plan. I'll give you tips about who to speak to at the credit card company, what to ask, and what to say. You'll tell the truth, of course, but I'll help you craft and polish your message so that it gets your situation across effectively.

Credit counseling

I already mentioned talking to a therapist or counselor if you have a shopping addiction. Here, I'm talking about an actual credit counselor. I usually get a negative reaction from readers when I suggest this. You can relax. I'm not suggesting that you should go into a debt-management program; I'm merely suggesting that you at least take advantage of a free phone counseling session. You'll be able to tell a professional credit counselor about your debt and you might also get a review of your current budget. Sometimes, this is all you need to get going in the right direction.

It's easy to be so deep in the weeds of debt that you can't see any path that will help you escape. A call with a counselor can give you some direction and help you weigh the alternatives.

I'll cover debt-management programs in Chapter 8 for those who feel they are too far in debt to even create a plan on their own. Let me tell you that there's no shame in this. You do whatever it is you need to do to fix your life, and I'll be here to cheer you on. Seriously, contact me via my Website and let me know how you're doing. I love to hear on-the-way-to-success stories!

Mistake #9: You Don't Have Any Financial Goals

There's something about keeping your eye on the financial horizon that changes the way you handle your money. It gives you a goal to work toward. And really, we all need goals, whether it's to own your own home, start an online business, or have an emergency fund that covers six months' worth of expenses.

Here's an example of how a financial goal can keep you focused. Let's say you want to own a home someday. But you're currently in $24,000 of credit card debt. In Chapter 7 we'll talk about how to use goals to keep you motivated. But just for fun, and to show how effective it is to keep your goals front and center, let's talk a little about it now. Ask yourself some questions: What type of house do you yearn for? Is it brick or stucco? Is it on a cul-de-sac? If you have kids, you'll probably try to get a house in a neighborhood that has a good school system. You'll have to think about how much you can pay in property taxes, too.

Find a photo that's similar to the type of house you want to buy when you're out of debt. In fact, if decorating is your thing, you can even start collecting paint chips and fabric swatches. Pinterest is awesome for this. I have some home décor boards, and I have pinned enough decorating projects to keep me busy for the next five years or so. If you prefer a hands-on approach, get a bulletin board and have at it. Or, if you want your home to have a home theater, start a folder on your computer, and bookmark research and the latest gizmos that theater junkies lust after.

Your goal list, along with the visual details, will help you stay on track. Let's say you're halfway to your goal and you have the sudden urge to go to the beach. Stop right there! Look at your goal list and remind yourself what you get at the end of all of the sacrifices you're making right now. Did you write down that you want to be in a position to buy a home in five years? Okay, that means you have something to look forward to. You have a goal that you can visualize and a reason to stick to your budget.

Speaking of which, sooner or later everyone gets tired of their budget. You start trying to convince yourself that your decade-old car stinks big time. You start to convince yourself that it's okay to buy a new car. You'll get back on track with your debt payoff as soon as you take this little detour. No, you won't get back on track. You'll be off track. It's different if your car is a threat to your safety. But if it's a case of getting antsy over being financially constrained, then take a look at the goals you've listed.

Once I finally had a list of financial goals, I stuck to my budget. Whenever I wanted to blow money on something I didn't need, I looked at my list. I had a condo on my list (thank goodness that one didn't work out!), an emergency fund, and a trip to Panama City, Florida. Florida was close enough to Atlanta to drive to, so it wasn't even an extravagant vacation. I once went on a cruise to Mexico when I had 10 cents in my checking account. No, I'm not kidding. I put this eight-day cruise to the Mexican Riviera on my credit card. I did this when I was afflicted with a bad case of head-in-sand syndrome. However, I really turned things around because my goals list kept me focused. We all need a little incentive when we have to go through hard times. It doesn't mean we're weak, just human. We'll talk more about how to set up goals and ways to stay on track in Chapter 7.

2

Look Your Debt in the Eye and Own It

Are you ready to do it? I think you are. I don't think you'd be reading this book if you weren't ready—or at least *close* to being ready—to own your debt. So much of personal finance is emotional. You have to be psychologically ready to tackle debt. You can't pay off debt until you acknowledge it and take responsibility.

If you still feel that you're a victim, you aren't ready to commit to the hard work of paying off your debt. Your anger and resentment will get in the way. So you can't blame the credit card company even if they raised your interest rate. And even if you got into debt through an unfortunate life circumstance, such as unemployment or medical bills, it's still your debt and you have to pay it off. Sometimes life isn't fair, but we still have to clean up the mess.

Here's the key: *Stare down your debt and it will lose its power over you.* You become the boss of your debt instead of the other way around.

Before we get into what it means to really and truly stare down your debt, let's take a look at another emotional issue that might be getting in your way.

Fear of Changing Your Lifestyle

This is a very real problem. Many who are in this situation don't have their heads in the sand. They know they're in a world of hurt. No one has to point it out because they are painfully aware of their situation. But they aren't ready to let go of the fancy restaurants and expensive cars.

Most people don't enjoy change because it's flat-out uncomfortable both emotionally and physically. Physically? Yup. I used to get terrible migraines every time I thought about tackling my debt. I'm prone to migraines so that's how stress is processed by my body. Other physical symptoms can include stomach upset, indigestion, high blood pressure, tension-related muscle pain, insomnia, and more. The brain is a powerful thing, and when we're stressed out, there's a physiological response as well as an emotional one. You can experience physical symptoms before you even take psychological ownership of your debt. It's always there in your subconscious, lurking in the shadows of your brain and creating stress.

Resistance to change is one of the major reasons why folks are slow to owning their debt. If you look at your debt numbers, then you probably should do something about it, right? It's okay to feel this way. Believe me, once you face it, it's hard to go back to denial. You likely won't want to go back to that state of mind anyway.

Taking action to pay off your debt means change. You might have to think about your lifestyle and cut some corners. I'm going to make you a promise right now: When you start seeing your total debt decrease, you'll feel great about all the temporary sacrifices you decided to make. And remember that's what this is: a temporary change. I won't lie to you: Some of your changes will need to be permanent, but there are some changes you'll make during the debt-reduction process, such as decreasing your entertainment budget, that you can kiss goodbye once your credit card balances are zero.

For instance, I ate tons of peanut butter and jelly sandwiches when I was paying off debt. Night after night. You can bet I didn't eat peanut butter again for a long time after I got out of debt. But when someone gave me a Christmas stocking full of miniature peanut butter cups a few years later, my boycott of peanut butter ended. Who can say no to chocolate and peanut butter?

So yes, change is afoot, but you won't be sacrificing everything that you love, either. Is your latte an essential part of your morning routine? If so, then keep your latte. My coffee ritual is set in stone, and no one is going to tell me I waste money on coffee. I like Starbucks coffee, which isn't cheap. But I grind my own beans and brew it in a French press. That first cup every morning is a great start to my day. But because I spend money on coffee, I cut corners in other places to pay for it. So I budget for my little coffee splurge.

This is what I call a budgeted splurge, and we'll cover this in Chapter 4 when we're putting your budget together. But for now, you don't need to worry about it or take immediate action. In fact, I want you to take plenty of time to think about your debt and what you should do about it. When people jump into a solution before they're ready, they have a greater chance of failing. And you're not going to fail. You're going to succeed!

Starting with your most recent credit card statements, we're going to do this in four simple steps, one at a time:

- Step 1: Just say it.
- Step 2: Stare down your debt.
- Step 3: Identify spending triggers.
- Step 4: Stop using credit cards.

Again, you will not be making any major decisions about your expenses or you budget in this chapter, so just relax and go through each step.

Step 1: Just say it.

Now's the time to acknowledge that you created the debt and you're responsible for getting rid of it. Fill in the blank with the exact amount and say it with me: *I've got _____ dollars of credit card debt and it's my job to pay it off.* I'm not kidding about saying it out loud. That makes it real. If it feels weird to say this to an empty room, then tell your dog/cat/hamster/fish you have $22,593.47 of credit card debt and it's your job to pay it off.

Now, if you have a significant other, but the debt is yours, let your partner know that you are taking responsibility. Hopefully your partner or spouse will be supportive, as that will be a big advantage for you emotionally. But there's another situation where owning up to your debt can get dicey.

Having debt as a couple

If you created the debt as a couple, then look each other in the eye and take responsibility for the debt together. Accumulating debt as a couple gets tricky when you decide to tackle it. If you're in a situation in which your significant other is still in denial (or worse, blaming you), then your first step is to get on the same page. This may not be easy, so if you hit a roadblock, get some marriage counseling to work out the issues. Otherwise, you won't make any progress. As your debt grows, thanks to compound interest, your marriage will likely suffer from the stress. A recent study from Kansas State University found that fighting about money was the biggest cause of divorce. The study also showed that it took couples longer to recover from fights about money than from fights about other topics (source: Dew, J., Britt, S. and Huston, S. (2012), "Examining the Relationship Between Financial Issues and Divorce." *Family Relations*, 61:615–628. doi:10.1111/j.1741-3729.2012.00715.x. School of Family Studies and Human Services, Kansas State University, Manhattan, KS 66506). So if you're in a money tiff with your partner, don't pretend it doesn't exist. Do what it takes to repair your relationship and your bank account.

Step 2: Stare down your debt.

Okay, you've taken the first step by acknowledging that you're responsible for your debt. That step alone will lift your attitude just a tad. You know why? Because it shows courage. Nothing lifts your spirits like showing the world you're ready to kick some debt butt. You're going to take the empowered approach to paying off debt. You say you don't feel powerful at the moment? Well, that's understandable. It's totally normal to feel that way at this stage of the game.

You might even be feeling a combination of depression and fear. It seems like a long road ahead. The length of the road depends on how much debt you have and how much cash flow you have to work with. But I hear you. No one wants to face it, because when you do, you have to take action. And we've already talked about how action leads to change, and that can be mighty uncomfortable.

But that's why I wrote this book for you. You don't have to do this by yourself. You've got me to cheer you on. Once you get moving and start shaking off the get-out-of-debt doldrums, you'll start to feel better. I know it's hard to believe, but you'll see what I mean once you start making progress.

The credit card debt worksheet

On page 50 you'll see a table, an example of how the worksheet will look when it's filled in. As you can see, you can list each of your debts. Even if you only have one credit card with a balance, you still need to list it so you can stay focused on the task at hand.

I also have a version of this worksheet available on my Website, *www.beverlyharzog.com*; you can download it for free. With the downloaded version, you can automatically rearrange the debts and play with the variables. The sample worksheet on page 50 has some credit cards and balances listed to show you how it should look. Of course you can always create your own spreadsheet or simply draw a table on a piece of paper, but you'll miss out on the bells and whistles I've added for your debt-reduction pleasure. But the theme of this book is to customize your debt plan, so if you prefer paper and pencil, go for it!

With the downloaded version, you can sort the debts in three different ways:

1. By APR, to pay your debt from highest interest rate to lowest.

2. By outstanding balance, if you want to start by paying off the smallest debt first.

3. By payment history. You're probably thinking, *Huh?* Well, if you've missed a payment, that debt gets priority no matter what the APR or balance might be. You're going to take action ASAP to reduce the risk of your account going to collections.

Fill in the worksheet with every credit card debt you have. Get the most current information from your paper credit card statements or, better yet, from your accounts online. So get your worksheet in front of you and let's fill this baby in.

CREDIT CARD DEBT WORKSHEET

Credit Card	Balance	Interest Rate (APR)	Minimum Payment	Due Date	Credit Limit	Utilization Ratio	Payments Current?	Over Credit Limit?
Discover	$1,500	14.0%	$32.50	8/20/14	$7,500	20%	No	No
Capital One	$7,000	22.0%	$198.33	9/29/14	$9,000	78%	No	No
Chase	$2,500	16.0%	$58.33	9/9/14	$9,000	28%	No	No
Wells Fargo	$3,000	11.0%	$57.50	9/4/14	$4,000	75%	No	No
Total	$14,000		$346.16		$29,500	47%		

Today's Date   12/2/2015

Instructions:
1. Enter the information in gray.
2. If you're using the version on *www.beverlyharzog.com*, the last three columns will be calculated for you.
3. Sort the columns to make your decisions.

If you aren't used to checking your accounts online, don't fret. But I will insist that you learn how to do this, because you should be checking your accounts several times a week to make sure there aren't any fraudulent purchases. Security breaches are becoming more and more common these days.

This recently happened to me—not with a credit card, but with a debit card, when my family went to Cocoa Beach, Florida, this past summer for vacation. While we were on vacation, the joint checking account that my husband and I share was hacked. We have several different accounts because we're both self-employed, so we diligently check our accounts every day. It sure is a good thing we still did that even though we were on vacation. On the way home from Florida, we stopped in Valdosta, Georgia, a lovely town in South Georgia, to grab a bite. My husband eats really quickly, so while the rest of us finished eating, my husband did the daily check on our joint account. He found $1,016 in fraudulent purchases.

He called our bank from the parking lot and told them what had happened. I really don't know how the debit card numbers got stolen, but we did get our money back after about 10 days. We then closed the account and opened a new one with very strong passwords. And that's something I am going to talk about briefly because of the account hacking that goes on. You must have strong passwords, and you must change them often.

Passwords 101

The most common passwords of 2013, according to SplashData, were "123456," "password," and "12345678" (source: *http://splashdata.com/press/worstpasswords2013.htm*). Seriously? I find these passwords amazingly lame. Please pick a strong password for each account to protect yourself. Yes, I know it's a hassle to have numerous passwords, but it's essential nowadays because hackers seem to be more sophisticated than ever. If you use the same password for all of your accounts, hackers will have access to all of your accounts if they figure out the master password. Think about that.

Here are a few tips for creating strong passwords:

- Use a combination of letters, numbers, and punctuation.

- Use random capitalization, and not just at the start of the password.

- Don't use your birthday, your significant other's birthday, your kids' birthdays, or any of their names.

- Don't use your pet's name.

Pet's name? Yes, because I'll bet you've mentioned your dog or cat or hamster on Facebook. I have a 5.5-pound Maltese named Marshall. He's insanely cute. It should be illegal to be this cute. That's why I upload his photos and talk about him all the time on Facebook. A fraudster who's tracking my social media would certainly try variations of "Marshall" while trying to hack into my accounts.

But I'm too smart for that and so are you. If you look through your previous updates on Facebook or on other social media, you'll probably be surprised at how much personal information you've revealed. Stalking people and monitoring their activities on social media is one of the most effective (and easiest) tools burglars and hackers have at their disposal. You're doing something very important for your future right now, and I don't want you to get sidetracked by identity theft. So don't make it easy for them. Strong passwords, people!

You can use a password manager to make it easier for you to keep track. Here are three popular password managers to consider:

- **Password Box:** Up to 25 passwords for free; you get unlimited password storage with Password Box Premium for $12 per year. Available for Windows, Mac, and mobile.

- **LastPass 3.0:** Free version available with great features, including a password generator; to get mobile access, you have to upgrade to the premium version for $12 per year. Available for Windows, Mac, Linux, and mobile.

- **Dashlane:** Free version available for a single device; for multiple devices, a premium version is available for $19.99; packed with features, including rating passwords and suggesting stronger ones and security breach alerts. Available for Windows, Mac, iOS, and mobile.

Your monthly statements

If you're just coming out of head-in-sand syndrome, you may not even know where your paper statements are. That's okay. As I mentioned earlier, we're going to look at your statements online anyway. And by the way, if you don't get online statements, also called eStatements or e-statements, consider doing so. Some credit card companies now charge for paper statements, so be sure you're not paying a fee for this. I have my statements sent directly to my inbox. It's better for the environment and it helps me stay organized. But if you're someone who has a paper file for everything from your kid's first drawing to the utility bill from 1994, then by all means, continue with what's working for you. If you've never checked them online, now's the time to set them up with really strong passwords.

Bring your account up on your computer. Then click on your most recent credit card statement and look at the details. Now go to your worksheet and fill in the information associated with that credit card. Now, don't freak out. Keep breathing. We're not making major decisions right now. No one is going to make you cancel cable. Not today, anyway! We're just getting a good, long look at the damage. That's all. If you need a box of tissues (or a bottle of wine or a six-pack), that's fine. Whatever it takes for you to get the nitty-gritty details onto the form.

Now let's look at each line of the worksheet that you need to fill in. So take a deep breath and type or write the following:

- Credit card name. Be specific. For example, if you have two Chase cards, write the full name for each card, like Chase Freedom card or Chase Sapphire card.

- Current balance.
- APR (interest rate).
- Minimum payment.
- Due date.
- Credit limit.
- Utilization ratio. This is the amount of your balance divided by your credit limit. Example: A credit card with a $500 balance and a $1,000 limit has a 50 percent utilization ratio (500/1,000).

Payments current? This requires a yes or no. If it's a "no," then this credit card automatically becomes your priority.

Follow this procedure for each credit card. If you have a credit card that has a balance of zero, I want you to write that down, too. We're going to make sure that credit card *stays* at zero. If you use it, you have to record it on this sheet and rework your numbers. What a hassle, right? You don't want to add to your debt once you have your debt escape plan in place.

Step #3: Identify your spending triggers.

We talked about nine mistakes in the first chapter that keep you mired in debt. Mistake #3 was not identifying the root cause of your debt. In other words, *what the hell led to this?* You need to identify how you got into this fix or it will probably happen again. So this step is crucial. I've noticed that a lot of personal finance experts like to compare overspending to diets. I can't think of a better one, frankly, so I'm going to piggyback onto to this and add my own spin.

The analogy goes like this: When you lose weight, you have to change your eating habits or you'll gain back the weight. Likewise, when you get out of debt, if you don't change your spending habits with your credit cards, you'll get into debt again.

Let's take the analogy further. Just changing your eating habits won't keep off the weight. You also have to exercise. You need to start planning your meals so you don't hit the drive-thru when you're too tired to go to the store. You also must identify your triggers for binging and then determine how to ambush them before they sabotage your weight loss. When it comes to getting debt-free, you do have to change your behavior, and you do that by identifying your spending triggers, or *spending catalysts*, as I like to call them. In other words, what makes you use your credit cards?

Back in my credit junkie days, I felt the need for new clothes, shoes, and fancy vacations. Notice I wrote "need." There was an emotional element to my spending, and it was tied to my self-confidence and self-esteem. These are two different issues, I know, but they often go together. When you have confidence issues, you often have self-esteem issues. And vice versa. When I had a bad day at work, which seemed to happen a lot because I hated my job, I'd go shopping for a quick pick-me-up. There was nothing like a new pair of heels in a fun color, like red, to boost my confidence. And then when I'd wear them to work, I'd get compliments on my new purchase. So, it was a double whammy for me. My purchases boosted both my self-confidence and my self-esteem.

Well, guess what? The adrenaline rush would fade, and then I'd have to go shopping again. I got caught up in a destructive cycle that led straight to credit card debt. When I finally hit rock bottom and took a look at my life, my self-confidence and self-esteem sank even further. But I knew I had to break the cycle and find affordable ways to feel better about myself and my life.

My root problem? It wasn't spending too much time at the mall. And it wasn't even an addiction to designer duds. It was the ego boost I got from wearing a new outfit to work. I worked on this issue while I was getting out of debt. I also decided I hated my job as an accountant and started doing some freelance writing. Once I was happier with my life, it was easier to change my spending patterns.

Think about what you spend your money on. The real problem is the trigger that creates the need to buy, say, home theater equipment you can't afford. Or maybe it's video games, cameras, expensive jewelry, furniture, or a car. A car? Don't laugh. If you have a high enough credit limit on a card, you can buy a car with it. I know someone who did that. Now, she was smart about it; she bought a car with a credit card that had a 12-month, 0% introductory offer. She made monthly payments (without having to pay any interest) and paid it off just as the intro period ended. But for those who are in debt, this is a terrible idea.

Sometimes the problem lies within our social circle. Do you go shopping with friends who shop as if it were a competitive sport? Or do you hang out with friends who go on lavish vacations they can't afford? One of my favorite sayings comes from Jim Rohn, an inspirational speaker: "You are the average of the five people you spend the most time with." This absolutely applies to spending habits. If you hang out with relatives, friends, or colleagues who practice reckless spending, then that becomes normal in your world. And you get approval from the group for having the same habits. We all take on some of the characteristics of those close to us. At the very least, we can be influenced by their behavior. I'm just throwing that out there so you can try it on and see if it fits.

It's almost never just one thing

There are few things in life that are truly black and white; most are varying shades of gray. So as you narrow down what, specifically, got you into debt, think about the other mistakes I mentioned in Chapter 1, too. Look beneath the surface and spend time thinking it through. Here's how this worked for me: I identified my spending trigger as "a bad day at the office." My career and my self-esteem were inextricably linked. They shouldn't be and they aren't now, but at the time they were. I shopped when I felt frustrated with my career, which was most of the time when I was in my 20s. My frustration often led to a crisis in confidence, which led to feelings of low self-esteem. Then, I made all the bad feelings go away with a new pair of red shoes.

I already mentioned that I committed all of the mistakes in the first chapter; at least, I did all of them to some degree. But what stands out for me the most are the following:

- Mistake #1: Head-in-sand syndrome led to more and more debt. I didn't feel confident that I could handle my debt situation, so I just pretended it didn't exist.

- Mistake #3: I identified the emotional element to my spending, but it took me forever to pinpoint how to fix my money problems. I had no budget and I didn't track my spending. I'll get to this problem in a minute.

- Mistake #4: I didn't make paying off credit card debt a priority. It took me a while to realize how much money I was wasting on interest alone.

- Mistake #8: I didn't know there was help out there. I didn't try to negotiate with my credit card companies. I went through it alone, and that made it tougher and more expensive than it had to be.

- Mistake #9: I had zero financial goals. Zilch. Oh, I thought about things I wanted, but I had no concrete plan to actually get there.

Okay, see how I did that? Emotional triggers are more difficult to fix, for sure. I'll tell you a secret. I said I never saw a credit counselor and that's true. But I spent about three years in therapy in my 20s. During that time, I never once mentioned my financial problems. Not one single time! Nope, I spent my one hour every three weeks talking about all the terrible dates I had. I kept attracting guys who were either unemployed or reckless spenders. I don't think that was a coincidence. I've heard that you tend to attract people who are on the same emotional level as you, and I think that works for your personal finances, too. Funny, once I fixed my credit problems, I started meeting more financially responsible men, one of whom became my husband.

But it's not all in your head...

It's all fine and dandy to work on your emotional triggers, but most likely you'll also have structural problems going on. I know that sounds bad, but these type of problems are much easier to fix than emotional issues. In Chapter 1, I talked about a lot of issues related to emotions that hold you back. No amount of structure in the world will keep you debt-free if you still don't know why you go shopping when you can't afford it. Once you get your head in the right place, then you can look at problems related to structure. Here's what I mean when I talk about structural issues:

- Not having a budget in place
- Not tracking spending
- Not having a savings account

For a few of you, the root cause may be totally structural. Once we get you set up with a budget and a way to track your spending, you might be close to breaking the chains of debt pretty quickly. But I urge you to go through the steps for honing in on your spending triggers, just in case you have a mild case of low self-esteem, a need to keep up with Joneses, or a need to be the first with the latest technology.

I'll bet you're starting to see how assembly-line debt strategies just can't work for everyone. That's why I wanted to write a book about debt reduction that didn't try to put a bunch of square pegs in round holes. There are so many ways to get *into* debt that we need at least a few different ways to get *out* of it!

Step #4: Stop using your credit cards.

Put down your credit cards and slowly back away. And put your hands behind your back. Just kidding! Not about stepping away from the cards, though. One of the benefits of staring down your debt is that you face the reality of what you have to repay. This helps your mind adjust to the idea of a credit-card-free lifestyle until you're out of debt. You simply can't make progress reducing your debts if you're continually adding to it.

And if you keep adding to your debt, you can't possibly make any progress on your credit score. In the coming chapters you'll see how it's possible to improve your score while you're getting out of debt. You'll be able to use your cards again once you're debt-free. But if you've decided that credit cards in general are your spending triggers, then you might decide it's best not to use credit cards at all. In fact, there are a lot of people who decide that credit cards just aren't for them. Jackie Beck, the founder of Thedebtmyth.com, made that decision. Here's what Jackie says about the decision she and her husband made:

My husband and I paid off over $147,000 in debt, and about $52,000 of that amount was consumer debt. What worked for us was changing the way we saw debt. We decided that debt wasn't a tool, it was a trap, and we were never going to be trapped by it again. Once we made a new habit of only buying things with money we already had—no matter what we wanted to buy—our lives changed for good. Behavioral change takes time, but it absolutely works long-term.

Jackie waited years before using credit cards again. And even when she does use them, she already has the money in the bank to pay the bill in full when it arrives. But if you decided never to use credit cards again, that's fine. While I do believe that debt can actually be a tool if used the right way, because it gives you a strong credit score, it's not my job to tell people how they should think or how they should behave when it comes to credit.

This book is about crafting the debt-escape plan that works for you. My goal is to help you make the decision that keeps you out of debt. What's right for you and me isn't necessarily the right decision for your BFF or your brothers and sisters.

And that leads us to the next stage, which I think you'll enjoy.

What is your relationship with money?

Do you like quizzes? I think most of us do. I can't tell you how much time I've wasted taking quizzes on Facebook or BuzzFeed. I know what kind of car I would be (expensive sports car), what dog I would be (cute mutt), what country I'm supposed to live in (New Zealand), and what *Friends* co-star I am most similar to (I admit that I'm as OCD and competitive as Monica).

In the next chapter, you're going to dig down deep into your psyche and answer 10 questions. Your responses will give you insight into what debt-reduction method you should use, how to motivate yourself, what method you should use to track spending, and a whole lot more. It's going to be fun!

3

What's Your Money Personality?

I think I love quizzes because I get a kick out of seeing what categories I fall into. Not because it changes my life in some profound way, but because it makes me think a little bit about life in general. And quizzes are also a fun way to procrastinate when I'm working, if I'm totally honest. In this case, we're going to use a quiz to find out what your money personality is.

The Money Personality Quiz

When I started thinking about what was wrong with a one-size-fits-all approach to debt elimination, I decided to create a quiz that would explore how people really feel about money, credit, and debt. We're all unique and that's what makes us special. I don't want you to change your personality to fit into a specific approach. For one thing, you're just fine the way you are. For another, it won't work.

Oh, you might make progress, but you might not make it all the way to total debt elimination.

There are two parts to this quiz. Part 1 is about your relationship to money. I created the quiz based on my many years of working with consumers, and helping them with their money and credit issues. I've seen definite patterns when it comes to personality and money management. Part 2 explores your learning style. This might seem a bit odd in this context, but stick with me and you'll see the connection. I've created a quiz based on the official VARK Questionnaire. The theory behind it is based on the VAK/VARK learning style model proposed by Neil Fleming in 1992. This model identifies four discrete learning styles, which describe how you tend to take in information: Visual (V), Auditory (A), Read/Write (R), and Kinesthetic (K).

The learning styles aren't just about classroom learning; they are also about processing and using information effectively. We're going to use your learning style to help you design your debt-escape plan. When you see the results of the quiz, you'll have a much better idea of how to set up your plan so that you will succeed. Trust me, you'll love the way this all comes together!

Part 1: How You Really Feel About Money and Debt

#1: You lost your job; the first thing you do is:

(a) Double-check your emergency fund to confirm that you can go six to eight months without an income. Thank goodness you have this safety net!

(b) You recently wiped out your emergency fund to take a Caribbean vacation. You'd planned to replace the money, but you kind of forgot about it. Your next move is to cry hysterically while hiding under the kitchen table.

(c) You scan your budget and change it so you don't spend a dime more than necessary. You only buy the necessities until you get a new job. You have an emergency fund, but it's $1,500 and that barely covers the rent. You wonder how many different ways you can make Ramen noodles taste interesting.

(d) You'll worry about how you'll pay your bills later. In the meantime, this has been a depressing day, so you go out for a steak and lobster dinner with friends. When the bill comes, you whip out your credit card, telling yourself you can pay the bill when you get a new job.

(e) You check all of your accounts: emergency fund, checking, savings, money market, mutual funds, and 401K. You think you have plenty of money to survive this, but you're not sure. What if you have a health crisis? What if you can't find another job?!

#2: Your uncle passed away and left you $5,000. You decide to:

(a) Deposit it into your child's college fund. You want to make sure she never has to take out student loans.

(b) Invest $3,500 in a mutual fund. You spend the remaining $1,500 on needed home repairs.

(c) Take the money gladly, even though you never liked this uncle. You'll deposit it into your checking account the next time you're near the bank. You think about trying to deposit by taking a photo with your phone, but you aren't sure how that works.

(d) Take the entire $5,000 and put in your savings account. You haven't had a vacation in a few years and you don't have debts to pay off, but you don't want to waste this godsend.

(e) Spend $1,000 on a much-needed beach vacation with friends, and another $1,000 on new clothes that you really need. Another $1,000 goes into your checking account for bills. You use the remaining $2,000 to pay toward your $5,000 credit card balance.

#3: You're out running errands and notice a sale at [insert your favorite store here], so:

(a) You can't resist going into the store to check out the goods. You don't plan to buy anything—well, unless you see something that's perfect. Or close to perfect.

(b) You bring up your budget on your smart phone to see how you're doing this month. If you have room in this category, you'll go in. If you don't have room, you'll keep walking.

(c) Of course you go in. Life is too short to ignore a sale. You're pretty sure you have room on one of your credit cards.

(d) Why would you go in? Just because you love the store doesn't mean you're willing to part with your hard-earned money.

(e) You're a little tempted, but an item from this store doesn't fit in with your spending plan for the month. You walk past the store, feeling confident about your self-control.

#4: When it comes to planning for your retirement, your philosophy is:

(a) How old do you think I am? I'm not worried about it right now. I have plenty of time to worry about that when I'm actually older.

(b) I'm all set unless something terrible happens. I save everything I can to prepare for it, but I still worry about it a lot.

(c) I have a diversified portfolio with mutual funds, IRA, and high-yield savings accounts. It should be more than enough, but I continue to save for it.

(d) I have a 401K and I contribute regularly. I also have a savings account and I'm careful about my spending, so I'm hoping it will be enough when the time comes.

(e) I know I should save for retirement. And I will, as soon as I can manage to stick to a monthly budget.

#5: Your monthly credit card statement shows up in your inbox. What's your next move?

(a) I don't use credit cards very often, so the bill is usually zero.

(b) I'm not sure what you mean by that. I don't even read my e-mails.

(c) I pay the bill in full using automatic bill pay. I know exactly how much I spent and where I spent it.

(d) I look at the minimum payment and I check the line items to see what I bought. I either pay the bill in full or carry the balance if I overspent that month.

(e) I schedule payment a few days before the due date via automatic bill pay. I don't take chances with payments.

#6: You just found out you need to replace your roof. The cost is $8,500. What's your strategy for paying the bill?

(a) You'll put it on your credit card. It will max out your card, but it's the only way you can pay for it right now. When the bill comes, you'll pay off $1,000 of it with your emergency fund. You wish you had a bigger emergency fund.

(b) You hate taking money out of your emergency fund for this, but there's no way you'll consider putting it on a credit card. You use your emergency fund to pay the bill in full and then start cutting expenses in your budget so you can replace the money as soon as possible.

(c) You put the expense on the credit card that offers the best rewards. Then when the bill comes next month, you'll pay it in full from your emergency fund.

(d) You get estimates from five more roofing contractors and manage to negotiate the cost down to $8,000. You pay the bill with money from your emergency fund. You consider toasting your brilliance with a cheap bottle of champagne, but in the end, you decide not to spend the money.

(e) You can't believe this has happened to you. You only have about $150 in your emergency fund, so you decide you have to put the roof on a credit card. You decide not to worry about it until the credit card bill arrives.

#7: A close relative needs to undergo a life-saving medical procedure. Unfortunately, your relative has a very high deductible on his health insurance and can't afford to have the procedure unless he gets some financial help. Your reaction is:

(a) You do what you can for family. You'll contribute $50 and hope all the other relatives do the same. That minimizes the amount each person has to contribute.

(b) You get a $1,000 cash advance on a credit card and contribute the money to your relative. Your heart's in the right place, but you have no idea you'll be paying 25 percent interest on that cash.

(c) You want to help, but you're already having problems with cash flow this month. You're sure you can help next month, and you call friends and relatives to find someone who can lend you a few hundred dollars so you can make a contribution.

(d) You have a category in your budget for charity. This seems like a good use of the money you had budgeted for this year. You even have enough money left to send flowers.

(e) You organize a family meeting so you can determine how much each person needs to contribute. You hope each person can contribute equally so no one has to carry the load.

#8: Do you know what your credit-utilization ratio is?

(a) You're not sure, but you think it might have something to do with your last physical.

(b) You know exactly what is and recalculate every week to make sure it's way under 30 percent, preferably closer to 10 percent.

(c) You rarely use your credit cards so you know your ratio is very low. It worries you if it gets above 5 percent.

(d) Of course you know what it is. You keep your ratio under 10 percent to maximize this part of your credit score. A high credit score helps you save on health insurance, car insurance, mortgage rates, and more.

(e) You've heard if it and you think it's supposed to be low, but you aren't sure why it's important.

#9: Your rent (or your mortgage) just went up by $300. The first thing you do is:

(a) Swear loudly (WTH?) and go out for a drink with your pals to forget about your troubles.

(b) Bring up your budget on your computer and change the total for your rent. You'll spend the next hour deciding where to find an extra $300. You decide to cut back $50 on groceries, $150 on entertainment, and spend $100 less during the holidays.

(c) You look at your budget and decide that you'll have to reduce your "cash leftover" amount every month by $300. Yikes.

(d) You freak out a little even though you have plenty of cash left over every month. You go through your budget and start reducing expenses.

(e) You make over your budget to accommodate the additional $300 expense. You'll reduce groceries by using more coupons and you'll use public transportation to save on gas costs.

#10: The thought of carrying a balance on your credit card and paying interest expense makes you want to:

(a) Throw up. And then throw up some more.

(b) Laugh derisively at the mere suggestion because it would never happen to you.

(c) Pay the minimum payment. And then figure out how to pay down the debt.

(d) Is that bad? I don't understand the question.

(e) You have great credit, so you apply for a zero-percent balance transfer credit card and pay the debt off during the interest-free period. You get out of debt and don't pay any more interest while doing so.

Scoring: Add up the points based on your answers.

1. a=2, b=4, c=1, d=5, e=3

2. a=1, b=2, c=5, d=3, e=4

3. a=4, b=2, c=5, d=3, e=1

4. a=5, b=3, c=2, d=1, e=4

5. a=3, b=5, c=1, d=4, e=2

6. a=4, b=3, c=2, d=1, e=5

7. a=3, b=5, c=4, d=2, e=1

8. a=5, b=2, c=3, d=1, e=4

9. a=5, b=2, c=4, d=3, e=1

10. a=3, b=1, c=4, d=5, e=2

Your score is between 10 and 17: The Clever Cheapskate

You're frugal and focused. You want to get more bang for your buck while spending as little as possible. You absolutely hate to waste money, and finding a bargain on a pricey item fills you with joy. You're not cheap in the sense that you're a tightwad. You're cheap as if it were a sport. If couponing were an Olympic event, you'd win the gold.

You research and plan events such as vacations to save money. You know the best Websites for deals and you don't mind spending hours searching online even if you only save a few dollars. You're smarter than most people and you use your brains to stretch a five-dollar bill until it screams for mercy. And then you stretch it some more.

Pluses: Diligently tracks spending and follows a budget; has a retirement fund and investment portfolio of conservative mutual funds; may or may not use a credit card, but never carries a balance; has a very nice emergency fund.

Minuses: Can be rigid when it comes to spending money on self, and that impacts how much life is enjoyed; can come across as cheap when giving gifts; has a hard time understanding when others feel the need to splurge (even a little bit).

Role model: Clark Howard

Your score is between 18 and 26: The Money Master

You're the wealth accumulator. You think a lot about the future. You're not afraid of it; you just want to plan ahead so your retirement is comfortable. You don't like to be in a position of being caught without enough money, so you have an enviable emergency fund.

You have a will and you've carefully considered who your heirs are (and who they aren't). You're always prepared financially because you pay attention to the details. You use a financial advisor, but you pay attention to what she's doing with your portfolio.

You use credit cards regularly for the rewards but you never carry a balance. You have a carefully crafted budget and you track your spending.

Pluses: Profits from credit cards; tracks spending and follows a budget; has a retirement fund that continues to grow; takes calculated risks with investments that pay off (most of the time); has a healthy emergency fund.

Minuses: Can be rigid when it comes to buying for others; often thinks so much about the future that the present isn't enjoyed; has trouble relaxing on vacation.

Role model: Warren Buffett

Your score is between 27 and 37: The Terrified Tightwad

You're the squirrel of the money world. No matter how many acorns you gather, it isn't enough. You differ from the Clever Cheapskate in a major way: You save because you're terrified you'll end up homeless. Your fears are probably rooted in childhood but to you they are very real. The Clever Cheapskate, on the other hand, isn't afraid and saves money as sport as well as to build a nest egg.

You're not a complete Scrooge because you can be generous when necessary. Collecting money is more about the need for security, and this means you want to stockpile as much money as is humanly possible.

Pluses: Self-sufficient and independent when it comes to money. If this person were a superhero, his/her superpower would be saving money and resisting impulse buys. Has a healthy emergency fund.

Minuses: Can annoy friends because when everyone splits the check at dinner, he/she will argue over who has to pay the extra penny if the math doesn't work out equally. Has a really hard time enjoying life in the present—especially if it involves spending any money—because of excess worry over things that might never happen.

Role model: A much nicer version of Ebenezer Scrooge

Your score is between 38 and 43: The Budget Buster

You actually do have a budget, but your best intentions are often undone by your impulsive purchases. You use credit cards and want to earn the rewards, but when you can't resist an item that's caught your eye, you bargain with the credit gods. You swear you'll cut corners somewhere else in your budget so you can buy the scarf or the Blu-ray player that's calling out to you from the shelf.

But then you kind of forget about your promise to the credit gods and you end up carrying a credit card balance and paying interest. You're working on an emergency fund and you hope to build a one in the future—just as soon as you pay off that extra debt you took on last month.

Pluses: Fun to be around and really does want to manage money responsibly. Has a budget at least, so is sometimes aware of overspending.

Minuses: Spur-of-the-moment purchases can wreak havoc on cash flow. Impulsive buying often leads to credit card debt.

Role model: Becky Bloomwood from the *Shopaholic* book series by Sophie Kinsella

Your score is between 44 and 50: The Unconcerned Consumer

You take a free-spirited approach to your money and to life in general. Deep down inside, you feel that life takes care of itself and things will just work out. You don't have a retirement fund, but you plan to think about it in your early 50s. Or your late 50s. Or something. You use credit cards with abandon, and it doesn't bother you if you carry a balance. Life is to be enjoyed, and you don't take compound interest too seriously. You don't have an emergency fund because you don't expect anything bad to happen.

Pluses: A lot of fun to be around and gives awesome gifts, although he/she can't afford any of them.

Minuses: Could end up having financially difficult later years due to the lack of planning and failure to build a retirement fund. Lack of an emergency fund is likely to create a financial disaster sooner or later, and the lack of a structured budget will lead to a mass of credit card debt.

Role model: Celebrities who personify conspicuous consumption (think the Kardashians)

Okay, now you're ready for the next step. You may be tempted to skip over this, but don't. You'll be amazed at how helpful this information will be when you're setting up your debt escape plan.

Part 2: How You Take In Information

I've always been fascinated by learning styles. There are many different models out there, but I like the work done by Neil Fleming, creator of the VARK model. I created a short quiz to help you figure out which learning style you tend to use. If you'd like to take the original 16-question quiz, you can find it at *www.vark-learn.com/english/page.asp?p=questionnaire.*

1. You are in charge of planning the family vacation. You:

a. Print out a photo of the resort and driving details.

b. Describe the activities in the area and what the resort is like.

c. Show them a map of the location.

d. E-mail or text links to the place you're considering.

2. You are preparing a birthday dinner for a close friend. You:

a. Know what you'll make and you don't need a recipe.

b. Call friends and ask for suggestions.

c. Get on Pinterest for ideas from the pictures.

d. Follow a favorite recipe.

3. You're watching a video to learn how to plant bulbs. What would be the most helpful to you?

a. Watching the gardener plant the bulbs.

b. Seeing diagrams and images.

c. Reading a bullet list on the screen.

d. Listening to an expert explain how it works.

4. Assuming price isn't an issue, what do you do when you want to choose a new non-fiction book?

a. You ask a friend for a recommendation.

b. You want the cover to be appealing.

c. You read the first several pages.

d. You like books that have anecdotes and examples.

5. You are in the market for a new smart phone. How would you make your decision?

a. You want a model that looks sleek.

b. You want the salesperson to tell you about its features.

c. You need to hold it and test it.

d. You go online and look at the features and reviews.

6. You're experiencing knee pain. At the doctor's office, what do you need to understand your diagnosis?

a. You need the doctor to tell you what's wrong.

b. You need a pamphlet describing your condition.

c. You need to see a diagram of your knee.

d. You need to see a model knee and have the doctor show you what's wrong.

7. Someone asks you for directions to a restaurant. You:

a. Show her a Google map on your phone.

b. Walk with her to the restaurant.

c. Write the directions on a piece of paper.

d. Tell her how to get there.

8. You bought a new video game and want to learn how to play. You:

a. Read the manual.

b. Talk to friends who know how to play the game.

c. Just start playing and figure it out.

d. Open the manual and look at the diagrams.

Scoring: Add up the points based on your answers.

1. a=3, b=4, c=1, d=2

2. a=4, b=2, c=1, d=3

3. a=4, b=1, c=3, d=2

4. a=2, b=1, c=3, d=4

5. a=3, b=4, c=2, d=1

6. a=4, b=3, c=2, d=1

7. a=1, b=4, c=3, d=21

8. a=3, b=4, c=2, d=1

Results: Count how many 1s, 2s, 3s, and 4s you have. If you have the most:

1s: you are Visual.

2s: you are Auditory.

3s: you are Read/Write.

4s: you are Kinesthetic.

We're all a little bit of a mix, but you'll probably find that your results show that you're strongest in one or two areas. Unless there's a huge gap between your strongest style and your second strongest, I'd consider using the top two as your primary learning styles.

My results showed that I process information as a Visual, but I also scored a few points in the Read/Write category. This tells me I relate to the world as a Visual, but my backup style is Read/Write. Not surprising, because

I'm a writer. I also noted that I didn't score well at all in Auditory. This made sense to me, too.

For example, while I'm working I can't listen to Pandora, which I usually love. I love music, but when I need to focus or understand something, I can't process music at the same time. You know how some people love a GPS system that talks to them? Not me. I can't listen to the instructions and process them. I prefer a map and written instructions on how to get somewhere. In my office I have giant whiteboards on the wall, which allow me to draw flowcharts or mind maps when I'm writing a book or even just trying to think through a blog post. I have lovely pale, mint green walls and an antique lamp that sits on a coffee table that was handed down to me by my mom. I've created a nice visual space in which to work, and tons of visual tools to help me do the work.

So that's how you can use your style to help you succeed in an important project, and getting out of debt is a *super*-important project.

Your Learning Style(s)

Let's take a look at each learning style, and I'll show you how to use your style(s) to your advantage while you're paying off debt.

Visual learners

You understand information better when it's presented in graphs, charts, maps, and the like. You like looking at infographics on the Internet. Being visual doesn't necessarily mean you take in information best via video. That may or may not be true. If the video has charts and graphs, you'll be engaged; if it doesn't, you'll be yawning.

What you need to include in your debt escape plan: Whiteboards that let you play around with mind mapping and counting down your debt, budgeting software that lets you view your budget in graphs and pie charts, vision boards with your debt goals, phone apps that offer striking visuals for tracking spending. Having a Pinterest board with your goals is a good idea. Index cards with a goal on each card works well for you.

Auditory learners

You take in information best by listening. You're the kid who could listen to the lecture and pass the test without further study. Auditory learners enjoy talking about things with friends. Some experts say that e-mail falls under the auditory umbrella, because e-mail messages tend to be written in a conversational style.

What you need to include in your debt escape plan: You'd enjoy learning about personal finance by listening to podcasts or to radio programs. In your debt escape plan, you'll need an outlet for talking about your goals and your progress. Getting involved in a debt forum where everyone becomes friends and cheers each other on might be helpful for you. Or you could put together your own e-mail "get out of debt" Yahoo group if you prefer a small community with folks you already know. Enjoy listening to music while you pay your bills and monitor your accounts.

Finally, choose software programs that are simple and not bogged down with too many frills and visuals. You won't read the directions and you'll get frustrated unless you have a natural technical ability.

Read/Write learners

You're the kid who could skip class, read the textbook, and still get a good grade. You connect with the world through reading and you remember what you've read. When you get on the Internet you often go from story to story without realizing how much time you've spent reading (raising my hand). You also enjoy writing and you're quite good at it. You basically love to learn.

What you need to include in your debt escape plan: You get a lot out of inspirational quotes, so having a Pinterest board with quotes can be an inspirational pick-me-up. Also try keeping a journal or writing a blog about your journey, or a notebook of what you'll do when you're out of debt. Read articles and books (like this one!) on personal finance to educate yourself.

When you choose a management software program, pick the one that suits your fancy. You'll be on the Internet learning all you can about it. You'll even read any online instructions you can find to maximize the use of the software.

Kinesthetic learners

If you go to the doctor for a knee problem, you prefer that the doc show you a model of a knee and explain what your problem is. If she just tells about your ACL tear, you won't understand it as well. You're a hands-on kind of person and you learn by actively engaging in an activity. If someone tries to tell you how to write a computer program, you need to actually do it on the computer to really connect with the information. You have a hard time sitting still for long periods of time, and if you work at a desk, you get up and walk around when you take breaks.

What you need to include in your debt escape plan: You might enjoy creating your own Excel spreadsheet for your budget and then creating pie charts and graphs. Regular physical exercise is important for everyone while working on debt reduction, but it's especially important for you. Using index cards to organize your debt reduction or goals is useful; just the act of shuffling the cards will help keep you interested.

Couples Who Have Different Money Personalities

This can be a real problem, especially if one of you is a Budget Buster and the other is a Clever Cheapskate. As I mentioned before when we talked about fighting about debt and marriage counseling, it's important to find common ground when it comes to finances.

So what if you're a couple and working on your debt together? If so, I applaud you for working together. Too many couples play the blame game when they get down to the nitty-gritties of paying off the debt. If you're in it together, that makes it easier. But if you're on opposite sides, you have a real problem. Often, I hear from folks who say that their spouse or significant other ruined their credit. If you have a joint account this is a real issue, and it's in your best interest to get legal help to protect yourself.

Now, if your problem is so serious that you're considering splitting up, I urge you to talk with an attorney. The advice in my book can help you if you're working together to get out of debt, but if you're at a point at which one person is gleefully ruining the other person's credit, then you *must* obtain legal help.

But hopefully the two of you are reading this book together, you both share the blame, and you both are ready to escape from your debt as a couple. And trust me when I say you'll feel like you're dating again when you get a taste of financial freedom. Even if you're opposite money personality types, if you've made a decision to pay off your debt, you can find a way to do it together. No one is a single, pure type. But if you really are that different, perhaps you have similar learning styles and can work together based on that.

If there really isn't any common ground, turn this supposed weakness into a strength. There's an economic concept called *comparative advantage*, which I learned about when I took international business in my MBA program. This means that a company makes business decisions based on what their strengths and costs are. So if a company can sell a widget at a lower cost (and make more money) than its competitors, it has a comparative advantage.

In the case of couples with divergent talents working to wipe out debt, each partner does what he or she does best. You're married to a Clever Cheapskate? This person is in charge of finding deals and keeping expenses as low as possible. If you're a Budget Buster, your job is to keep things upbeat and contribute a little whimsy. You might be surprised at what you can accomplish when you assign roles based on comparative advantage.

4

Be the Boss of Your Budget

Are you ready to break free from the chains of debt? You bet you are! If you weren't, you wouldn't have made it to this chapter. You would have come up with at least a dozen excuses as to why this wasn't the best time in your life to make difficult changes. You'd say that you needed to find a new job first, even though you haven't even begun to look for one. Or you'd pass the blame to someone else—your ex, the credit card company, your Chihuahua.

For now, just relax and read on. We're about to fix a problem that's been holding you back from financial freedom. I suggest you read through the chapter and not worry about making a decision. If you're new to budgets, I want you to soak up the information without the pressure of having to take action right away. Then, read it again with a more discerning eye.

The Not-So-Boring Basics of Budgets

I'm not kidding. This will not be boring. Stick with me here and you'll be on your way to the budget that will help you get out of your credit card debt mess. You've already made some strides toward getting out of debt. Well, you're about to feel a lot better because you're now going to make a *giant* step toward getting out of debt. First I'm going to describe different budgeting programs, and cover the highlights and the lowlights of each. Then I'll point out how your type and learning style might benefit from a specific program.

Here are a few things I want you to keep in mind while we talk about budgets:

The KISS (keep it simple, stupid) method rules. Simplicity rocks!

You'll want to track your spending for two to four weeks with pen and pad. Four weeks is ideal, but do two weeks at a minimum. This will help you determine where your money is going. You might be surprised at how much you're spending at Taco Bell.

Another option is to pull out credit card bills and receipts and see how much you've spent and in what categories. If you have all the receipts, I'm already impressed with you. But it's still a good idea to track your spending for a few weeks in case you don't save every single receipt.

You'll be adding up all your sources of income. Yours, your significant other's, your cat's. This can be tough to do if you're self-employed. If you run your own business, take a look at your income statements for the past year. Calculate your average income for each month. Be flexible, though, because a change in the economy might mean you need to change your estimates.

You must tell the truth. If you eat Chinese delivery four times a week, you've got to write that down. You can't make a decision about an expense until you've written it down as a current expense. Only you and your family members will see it. It might not be a pretty sight, but that in itself is motivating.

Stay flexible. Situations change, and sometimes your budget will need to change, too.

Get started with a simple budget worksheet

I've created a very simple budget worksheet in Excel for you to try. I was serious about keeping things simple. You can see an example on the following two pages. The sheet has sample numbers filled in so you can see how it works.

You also have the option to download the worksheet from my Website, *www.beverlyharzog.com*. That makes it easy to use as a budget tester. You can create new categories and enter the amounts, and the totals are calculated for you. You can play around with it while you decide what the numbers are now and what they need to be for you to start paying more than the minimum amounts on your debt.

If you aren't comfortable with adding your account information to Websites that offer free money-management software, feel free to stick with this. But you will have to manually add your expenses and keep track of things on your own. For some, that might be a good thing as long

BUDGET WORKSHEET EXAMPLE

	CURRENT AMOUNT	NEW BUDGET	DEBT ESCAPE
INCOME			
Earnings			
Job #1	$3,707	$3,707	
Extra Cash Flow		$60	$60
TOTAL INCOME	$3,707	$3,767	$60
FIXED EXPENSES			
Home			
Mortgage	$1,200	$1,200	
Property Taxes	$200	$200	
Emergency Fund	$50	$50	
Utilities			
Electricity	$200	$200	
Water	$30	$30	
Gas	$30	$30	
Internet	$50	$50	
Cell Phone	$50	$50	
Transportation			

Car Loans	$300	$300	
Auto Insurance	$50	$50	
Gas	$100	$100	
Health Care			
Health Insurance	$400	$400	
Prescription Co-Pays	$50	$50	
VARIABLE EXPENSES			
Home Maintenance	$50	$50	
Household			
Groceries	$400	$350	$50
Attire	$125	$100	$25
Home supplies	$50	$40	$10
School supplies	$50	$40	$10
Entertainment	$182	$132	$50
Health Care	$100	$100	
Grooming	$40	$25	$15
TOTAL EXPENSES	$3,707	$3,547	$160
TOTAL DEBT ESCAPE			$220

as you're diligent about tracking expenses. Keep a small notebook with you at all times or keep receipts.

Using this method is a good way to develop some self-discipline with your spending. You'll get tired of tracking it and you'll start to cut back on spending. Yep, this is the method I tried years ago to tackle my debt. It worked because it made me think about every penny I spent.

What are your current categories?

As I already mentioned, you need to track your spending for a few weeks in order to discover what your patterns are. You won't necessarily use every category you come across during the two weeks because, for some expenses, you'll be aghast that you wasted money on them. You'll decide right there to cut them out of your routine until you're out of debt.

Expenses come in two stripes: fixed and variable. The definitions are exactly how they sound. Your mortgage is a fixed expense. Your health expenses are a combination of fixed (insurance premium) and variable (you get the flu and have to visit the doc). Here are some category suggestions to get you going:

Spending categories: fixed expenses

Home: mortgage, rent, furniture, property taxes, repairs, landscaping, and insurance.

Utilities: electricity, water, gas, cable, Internet, land phone lines, and cell phones.

Transportation: car loan payment, car insurance, gas, bus passes, subway/train tickets, repairs, registration fees, and lease payments.

Health-related fixed expenses: Insurance premiums, dental visits, eye check-ups, contact lenses, life insurance premium, prescription medication, and gym memberships. (I put anything that helps you stay healthy in this category, and a gym membership does that.) If you don't have health insurance, that's a big variable expense you have to deal with.

Spending categories: variable expenses

Grocery expenses: Food for meals you eat at home go in this category, obviously. However, there are some things you buy at the grocery store that can also go into another category. For instance, disposable diapers and over-the-counter medications are nonfood items, but maybe you always buy them when you do your grocery shopping. You have two choices here: You can break down each type of nonfood expense as a separate line item in your budget, or just lump it all together as "grocery expense." Whichever way you decide to go, just be consistent. If you lump it all together, keep a list of the nonfood items that are included in this category for reference.

House-related variable expenses: furniture, property taxes, repairs, and landscaping.

Entertainment: restaurants, books, movies, subscriptions to Netflix and magazines/newpapers, concerts, travel, vacation, hobbies, and buying music.

Health-related variable expenses: co-pays on doctor visits, dental treatments, new eyeglasses or contacts because your prescription changed.

Personal expenses: shampoo, soap, clothes, shoes, jewelry, hairstylists, manicures, gifts, makeup, shaving cream, razors, and on and on. You don't have to list individual items. Just do an inventory of what you and your family's personal needs are.

Pets: grooming, boarding, food, checkups, training, and health emergencies.

Miscellaneous: This is a catch-all for unexpected expenses. For instance, a group of high school kids in my neighborhood were collecting school supplies for kids in Tanzania. I spent $27, which was more than I intended to, but it was for a good cause and I had the room in my budget that month. Another example is when you have unexpected houseguests and you need to spend more on food. You don't want to change your budget because it's a one-time thing. But you do have to account for the expense somewhere.

At the end of the day, if you have children you *really* need this category. What if your daughter suddenly decides she wants to play soccer, and you need to pay registration fees and buy shin guards? Stuff happens when you have kids—a lot of stuff!

Income sources

Work: Add up all sources of income from work activities *after taxes*.

Dividends, investments, and other sources: Look at statements and get a realistic view of what you earn each year. Consider tax implications in case you need a holding account set up for that expense.

Your money at the end of the month: This part is easy to do, but sometimes not so easy to look at. Here's the calculation:

Your total income – your total expenses = your net income

Are you "in the black" or the "in the red," as we used to say in my former CPA life? The budget you're working on right now is preliminary. You're establishing a starting point so you can make decisions about how you'll spend your money going forward. We need to know how much you spend now and how much is left over to get a realistic picture of your cash flow. Then we'll "massage" the numbers until you find the money to throw at your debt. Paying more than the minimum is how you get out of debt.

So get the numbers in place, but don't freak out. In a minute, I'll show you how to eliminate or just downsize an expense. And you'll even get ideas on how to increase your income a little in Chapter 5. And no, this doesn't mean working the night shift at your local Waffle House.

Two Rules for Success

Before we jump into the next phase, there are two rules you must follow from this moment forward. I'll keep it short and sweet. The first rule should not be a surprise.

Rule #1: Stop using credit cards.

I know I already said this, but I'm saying it again just in case you're skimming instead of reading. Relax—I'm not scolding you. I'm a major skimmer myself. But this is so important that it bears repeating. Before you go any further with your debt escape plan, you must commit to *no more credit card spending.* You can't pay off debt if you're trying to hit a moving target. If you aren't ready to do this, then you aren't ready to get out of debt. I'm pretty flexible on a lot of issues, but, darn it, this isn't one of them.

Now, if you need your cards to make ends meet, that's a different problem. Take a look at Chapter 8 to get some tips on how to proceed when you need to use credit cards to cover your basic needs.

Rule #2: Question every expense.

Look at the status quo with a new, more critical eye. Don't let any line item on your budget escape scrutiny. We often buy things because that's the way we've always done it. This can lead to mindless spending. Again, I'm not saying you have to cut cable. But maybe if you look at your Internet and cable service, you'll find some things you're not using. You might just find money in places you didn't expect to.

For example, two years ago I decided to review our insurance policies. I had two teenagers at the time, and auto insurance was expensive. One of them was a teenage boy and, let me tell you, insurance rates are high for that group. I found that we were paying more than we needed to. There were discounts we could get because my kids had excellent grades. When my son got his license a few years ago, out insurance company had a special program they wanted new drivers to take. By going through the program, which involved keeping a driving log, we saved on my son's insurance premiums.

If you have a child who has just left for college and who didn't take a car, you might be able to get a temporary reduction on her rates. These discounts all vary, of course, depending on the carrier. But the point is that you need to question every expense.

Even if you feel that your chances of "finding" money don't go beyond the loose change in the couch cushions, stick with me for a minute. When I was faced with paying off more than $20,000 in credit card debt, I felt demoralized and emotionally paralyzed at first. That's a rough combination to overcome. But I made myself go through my written-out budget with an eagle eye. There were some items that I took off my budget without having to think too much about it; it was that obvious to me. That was the "slash and burn" list, which is what you'll do next.

Okay, now that you've sworn to uphold the two rules you're ready for the next step: cutting back on your expenses. Hold your current budget in front of you. See the column on the far right where it reads "Debt Escape"? That's where you'll record the amount of money you "find" after you decrease or eliminate an expense.

Slash and Burn List

This is the list that should be a no-brainer for you. These are the expenses that you know you can and should give up, at least temporarily, while you're getting out of debt.

Here's what I had on the cutting room floor: clothes, shoes, and expensive makeup. I had more than $20,000 worth of clothes and shoes, so I didn't need anything else in that category. And I switched to inexpensive makeup, which was a big sacrifice for me. I've always been a girlie girl, so makeup has always been a big deal to me. Just so you know the extent of it, when I went into labor with my first child, I wouldn't leave for the hospital until I put on mascara and lipstick. That might sound fairly normal until I tell you that it was 2 a.m. and my contractions were just a few minutes apart. I barely made it to the hospital in time to give birth, but I looked great!

Downsizing Expenses

These are expenses that you can't eliminate entirely but can be reduced. This is a fishing expedition, so relax. As I already mentioned, you need to challenge your assumptions about your expenses. Sometimes we get on autopilot and we go about our business without questioning whether we could or should make changes. So explore each category and look at the ideas for money-saving opportunities.

Groceries

There are many ways to find $25 to $50 a month with groceries. Here are just a few ideas to get your creative juices flowing.

Start cutting coupons. I'm horribly inept with coupons. I love the concept, don't get me wrong. But I seem to have some kind of mental block when it comes to actually handing them to the cashier. I once paper-clipped a "$2 off" coupon for Advil to the front pocket of my purse and I *still* managed to forget to use it. So this is one of those suggestions where common advice works for some, but not for all. See? It's all a personal thing when it comes to success. Fortunately there are now tons of Websites and apps out there to make the process of saving easier. Check out these sites to start:

- *www.5dollardinners.com/category/coupons*
- *www.thegrocerygame.com*
- *www.couponsherpa.com/grocery-coupons*
- *www.thekrazycouponlady.com*
- *www.couponing.com*

Eat more-affordable food. If you enjoy red meat, maybe you could eat less filet mignon and more sirloin. Or take it down another notch and switch to lean ground beef for a while. You can also make casseroles that combine smaller amounts of lean meat with beans and vegetables. Anything with fiber is going to make you feel full.

I realize that I'm not telling you anything new here. But consider tweaking your diet just a tad so that you spend less and find $50 extra per month to throw at your debt. If you buy foods out of season, you'll pay more. This takes a little more planning, so if your schedule is already packed, you might decide to keep the status quo on food purchases and look for money elsewhere.

When I was getting out of debt I slashed my grocery budget and found about $250 a month that way. I ate a ton of peanut butter and jelly sandwiches and also took advantage of free buffets at bars that offered two-for-one drinks. It was the '80s and it was easy to find free buffets. I could go out on the town with friends for about $3 and go home happy.

The reason this worked for me is because I was single with no kids at the time. I could make any choice I wanted when it came to cutting my budget. I was lucky in that regard. But you might be contending with different circumstances. If I had had a husband and three kids at the time, well, that approach wouldn't have worked!

Cut back on unnecessary but enjoyable vices. Most of us enjoy a beer or a glass of wine or two with dinner. You don't have to cut out all the things you do to unwind, but reevaluate your choices and how often you buy them. I love a good pinot noir and I found one for $8 a bottle that I enjoy. Sure, I prefer a $20 bottle, but I can save that for a special occasion. Similarly, if you're buying cigarettes, well, I'm not going to judge you, but they aren't good for your financial health, either. Try to at least cut back, because that's an expensive habit.

About those lattes... I'd give up modern electricity before I gave up my coffee. I don't go out and buy $3 lattes because I like my coffee plain and freshly made. I use a French press and grind my own beans every morning. Sure, I could save money by buying less expensive brands, but I won't do that because I like Starbucks. I adore my morning coffee experience and it's an essential part of my day. So I keep my coffee splurge and cut corners elsewhere in my grocery budget to accommodate it. I don't buy soft drinks, I buy affordable wine, and I don't buy snack food.

So if you like your latte, you can keep your latte. But cut $3 a day from somewhere else in your budget to cover it. You can also consider a compromise. Get your lattes on weekdays, but make your own coffee on the weekend. The possibilities are endless, so do what works best for you and your budget.

Cut back on convenience items. Save money by shredding your own cheese, cleaning your own greens to make salads, and chopping your own broccoli. This approach might be a problem for those who rush home from work and have to feed hungry children as soon as possible. I remember those days; it's a juggling act, for sure. You want to give your kids a healthy meal, but you need to do it quickly so they can do their homework and take baths. Oh, and hungry kids are quite cranky.

So if you work and have children to feed, you probably can't function without these time savers. And if losing your time savers makes you eat out to get back the time, then this is a bad idea for you. That's okay. But for those who have the time, you can shave off some expenses right here. Now that my youngest just left for college, I have more time than ever to get dinner on the table. So I'm finally at a point where I can save money this way.

Use Pinterest to find affordable yet nutritious recipes. As a visual person this works for me. I can go to my boards and pick recipes for the week. I've made a point of collecting quick and fairly affordable recipes. Occasionally I'll buy scallops because I love seafood. But I also have a collection of easy-to-make, cheapo dinners such as chicken-and-noodle casseroles. I mentioned $5 Dinners as a resource for coupons, but it's also a good resource, not surprisingly, for inexpensive dinner ideas (*www.5dollardinners.com*).

Pay for meal plans. It may sound counterintuitive to suggest paying for meal plans in order to save money. But I've heard from folks who use eMeals and they say they save money on groceries.

You choose a meal plan from a variety of choices (low-fat, gluten-free, simple gourmet, and so on), and each week you receive a meal plan with a grocery list. You save time on planning and making a list. You also save money because you're using a list and not winging it at the grocery store. I'm actually considering using this for my own family. I love to cook, but the meal planning part of it can be a drag.

Reconsider your transportation. Do you pay a lot for parking? Do you *need* a car? Don't get mad at me for the last question; I'm just asking. If you have kids and live out in the suburbs, I realize you need a car or two for that lifestyle. But if you live in a major city on public transportation and it's just you and a partner, then maybe you can get by for a while without wheels.

If you work in an office and a few coworkers are nearby, consider carpooling, at least temporarily. If you're an introvert, you might cringe at the thought, but for extroverts, this might be a fun way to kick off the day. You'll save on gas expenses and decrease the rate of wear and tear on your car.

DIY and the Opportunity Cost

Hey, don't stop reading. I'm not going to get all economics-ninja on you. This is just an interesting concept and it relates to the best way to spend your time: the balance between saving money and wasting your time, on one hand, and having it cost you more in the long run, on the other.

I do want to say that this section isn't for everyone. If you're in the barely making-ends-meet group of debtors, then you're probably insulted that I even suggested that you might be wasting money on luxuries. So let me say that I know where you're coming from and I've been there. This section is for those who have debt but aren't desperate for cash flow. If you're in that category, then you can make some changes that could really put your debt-elimination plan into overdrive.

Here are some services some of us pay for that we could do ourselves: lawn maintenance, housecleaning, car washing and detailing, changing the oil in your car—things like that. If paying someone else to do these activities frees you up to make more money, then it's probably a good use of resources. But if it's just an "extra" you give yourself, then maybe you can forgo this expense until you're out of debt. Of course, some of these activities, such as changing the oil in your car, requires a little know-how, so you have to decide how much effort you're willing to put in to learn.

Lawncare

Put your kids to work. You can even pay them if you like. You'll save a bunch by converting this expense to a do-it-yourself experience. Full disclosure: I hire a lawn service because I live in a neighborhood with strict rules about lawn appearance. I use the time I'd spend on the yard at my desk working. Yes, it's an expense, but it frees me up to make money to pay my bills, and I do come out ahead in the end.

Housecleaning

Occasionally, I'll come across a blog where women and men are arguing about hiring a housekeeper. Usually the arguments are about whether you should feel guilty about doing this. I don't get this at all. If you don't have time to clean your house and you have the funds for this, then get a cleaning service. It's all about the opportunity cost, not the so-called guilt. But if you can skip this expense and you and your spouse can divide the chores for now, you'll save money. It also helps if you have a high tolerance for a less-than-perfect-looking home.

Car washing and detailing

I'm going to assume that you're probably not wasting your cash on fancy car washes. But just in case you are, this is a no-brainer. Your car can even get a little dirty while you're becoming debt-free. Once you're out of debt, you can write "Debt Free" in the dust and dirt on the back windshield before you drive over to the car wash.

Entertainment

You can really save a lot in this area. You just have to get creative. During the time I was paying off debt, I gave myself $10 a week for fun stuff. That was it. I know that sounds terribly cheap, but as I've already said, I didn't have kids. I also had an advantage because I was single and dating, so I was treated to meals pretty regularly. Don't judge me. It was a different time and place, and, believe me, I went Dutch often enough.

Cable and electronics. Do you *need* HBO or can you wait and watch *Game of Thrones* on DVD? If you just threw this book across the room, then I guess you need HBO! But you get my drift, right? Look at every cable, phone, and Internet package you have and see if there's some fat you can cut. And remember: the changes can be temporary. Really, I'm not lying!

Exercise

I consider exercise an essential activity when you're in debt. It's just plain stressful, and you need to take care of yourself. For one thing, you don't want to get sick and have to pay healthcare bills. You don't necessarily have to eliminate your gym membership if working out is important way for you to deal with your debt. I had an expensive health club membership, so I downsized to a cheaper alternative in my neighborhood. The towels were cheap and the atmosphere wasn't like a country club, but it got the job done. I still got to enjoy great aerobics classes, and that helped me deal with my debt-related stress.

If you can eliminate the expense simply by walking or jogging around your neighborhood, go for it. Exercise is an almost necessary activity when you're under severe stress, so try to fit it in. If you just decided to start exercising after reading this, check with your doctor and make sure you're healthy enough to work out. I don't want you getting injuries!

Common Things That Screw Up Your Spending Plan

I love holidays. Honestly, I'll celebrate anything. I enjoy making holiday-themed dinners and decorating for a special season, such as Halloween or even St. Patrick's Day. If you enjoy taking advantage of what every season or holiday has to offer, you have to be careful to watch your budget. Hopefully, you have the expense covered in your "miscellaneous" category, or maybe you have a separate category for Christmas or whatever holiday you and your family celebrate.

There are affordable ways to celebrate without busting your budget; sometimes you just have to think outside the box. Here are some suggestions based on what I've done in the past:

I once decorated for a Halloween party by using old costumes my kids had grown out of. I attached them to a wall and it was a glorious display of princesses, skeletons, and goblins from years past.

Over the years, I've turned anything and everything into a Christmas tree ornament. My son's candle from his first birthday cake? Check. The tiny birdhouse my daughter made in Girl Scouts? Check. Our tree is a memory tree, and though it isn't gorgeous, it's full of life and character. And it was inexpensive to create.

On Thanksgiving, instead of footing the bill for the entire family's meal, offer to make the turkey and the stuffing and assign side dishes and desserts to others. My parents are both gone now, but over the years this approach saved me and my sister a lot of money. It's less stressful for the host, too.

Have a birthday party at home instead of an expensive location. This may take finesse on your part because there's awful pressure these days to have a "statement" or "theme" birthday party. I once had an "anti-theme party" for my son's 6th birthday. I set up play stations around our house and each one had a different focus. I had a Lego station, a dinosaur station, an outdoor bug hunt activity, and so on. The kids were engaged and loved it.

See what I mean? If you give it some thought, you can still enjoy special occasions without emptying your pockets. While you're paying off debt, it's essential to stay on track with your spending plan. On my Website you'll find a holiday spending worksheet that I've put together for you. You can use this to track your spending manually; or, you might opt to use a spending app, which I've listed in the resource section in Appendix B.

5

(Almost) Pain-Free Ways to Increase Your Income

I can't lie to you. There's a little bit of pain involved in a few of these strategies, but the pain is a whole lot less than the pain of enduring debt, day after day. Anything that gets you even one day closer to being debt-free is worth the effort.

Still have your simple budget worksheet in front of you? Look in the income section over to the right and you'll see a spot to pencil in the increased cash flow you find. When you add the "found" money from slashing your expenses to your cash flow boost, you'll get your **debt escape number**. This is the number you'll add to the minimum payment of your target debt.

Know Thy Credit Score

I go into more detail about FICO scores in Chapter 7, but I want to mention a few basic things here before we talk about your debt-reduction and cash-flow-boosting options. For instance, with balance transfers, you need to know your credit score before you proceed.

I don't want you to get upset if your FICO score is in the toilet. You're not alone. Plenty of others are in the same boat. And remember that a bad score can be fixed. Above all things, keep that little nugget in mind: *You are not doomed forever.*

Your FICO score, though important, is simply a barometer of your credit health. And there are many different credit scores, by the way. But for our purposes, I'm focusing on FICO scores, and you should, too. About 90 percent of lenders use a variation of a FICO score model. Other scores, such as VantageScore, have educational value, though, and that's why I often suggest that getting your free score from a Website is a good way to monitor your credit health.

Knowing your baseline credit score is essential. This tells you up-front what the options are (and aren't). For example, if you still have excellent credit, getting a balance transfer credit card is a real possibility. If your score is below average or even poor, then you don't need to waste time on it. I'm all about making this easy for you. (Canadian readers should note that the system in Canada is pretty similar to that in America, although the credit bureaus and associated organizations obviously have different contact information. For more on this, see Appendix B.)

Before we get to FICO scores, let's take a look at the free route. They're what are called FAKO scores (other than the free FICO scores offered by a few issuers), or educational scores, but they have value as well.

How to Use Free Credit Scores

There are three different sites that I've personally used and can recommend: Credit Karma, Credit Sesame, and Credit.com. Another site I haven't tried yet is WisePiggy. com. I've heard good things, though, and I like the resources available on that site. Now, you do *not* get FICO scores from these sites, but you do get an educational score that you can use to gauge your progress. In other words, you get a general picture of credit health, and that's a valuable tool.

You can't take these scores and compare them to FICO scores. Credit Karma offers your TransUnion credit score (from TransUnion) and a VantageScore. Credit Sesame uses the Experian National Risk score, which comes from Experian. Credit.com offers VantageScore 3.0 and Experian's National Equivalency score.

I'd choose one site and follow that score to see how you're doing and gauge your progress. I signed up for scores on all three sites when I was writing *Confessions of a Credit Junkie*, and my scores were all wildly different. That'll just confuse you and it won't give you an added benefit.

No matter which site you choose, here's how to get value from these freebies:

- You'll get a grade for different factors that go into your score. For instance, you might get an A– for payment history.

- Read the comments and suggestions for each factor because that's where the most value lies.
- Don't buy the credit monitoring services that are offered on the sites. You'll see a hard sell for this service or for an identity theft monitoring service; in most cases, you don't need the extra expense.
- Don't buy credit reports from any of these sites. You can get your official credit reports for free right here: *www.annualcreditreport.com/index.action*.

If you're a customer of a few select group of credit card companies, however, you might not need these free sites.

Hell finally froze over

I didn't think I'd live to see the day when credit card companies started offering free FICO scores. You can see your FICO score on your monthly statement. Remember: your FICO score here is only a snapshot, and there's a time delay between the time you see it and the time it was calculated. But there's not much of a delay, so it's still a valuable resource.

As of this writing, the three credit card companies that offer this benefit with some of their cards are Discover, Barclays, and First Bank National. Citi has announced that they will be offering free FICO scores online for customers with Citi-branded cards in January 2015. The credit card industry is highly competitive, so I wouldn't be surprised to see more issuers offering a free FICO score in the future or, at the very least, devising their own way of competing with those who do.

Capital One offers a Credit Tracker score that gets information from your TransUnion file. But it's not a FICO score; it's an educational score. Still, it's free, and if you have a Capital One credit card, it might be a convenient way to monitor your general credit score progress.

How to Use Paid FICO Scores

You can buy your FICO Score on myFICO.com, which is a great resource for learning more about how your score is calculated. This Website has recently changed its home page; the first thing you see is a push to buy their combo platter: a service to monitor your FICO scores and identity for $29.95. If you think you can sign up for this to get the free scores and then cancel the service, think again. There's a three-month minimum requirement, and, from what I can tell, there is no free trial period. So you'd get three scores for $89.85. You do also get the monitoring service, but you don't need that unless you're in a situation such as a contentious divorce (and you have a joint account) or you're having problems with identity theft.

Click on Compare Our Products and scroll down to where you see "FICO Standard." You can select the FICO Standard score from one of the bureaus; it's $19.95 for each score. You can get your FICO standard score pulling information from Equifax, TransUnion, or Experian. Just pick one to get a starting point for your FICO score.

I still love this site for the educational value, but I'm not happy that they've made it confusing to buy their least expensive and, in my humble opinion, most valuable product—the FICO scores. So be careful about what you're buying. To skip all the product hoopla, go to this Web page: *www.myfico.com/products/ficoone*. You're welcome!

There's an option to buy all three scores for $59.85, but there's no savings to you to buy all three at once, so don't do it right now. That would waste your money when you're not sure if you even need all the scores. Besides, these scores change whenever new information comes in about your payment history. You're looking for a snapshot of your credit score, not a scrapbook of all your scores. So it's actually a good idea to spread this out a little if you do decide you want to check all three.

What your FICO score tells you

You need to know your FICO score so you can decide what strategies are available to you for your debt escape plan. For instance, a balance transfer is a good idea if you have a very good FICO score. What's very good? Well, 700 to 749 is considered good and 750 to 850 is excellent. To qualify for the best balance transfer card offers, you'll need about a 720. But even if you're closer to 700, you still have options. We'll talk more about that in the next section.

Now, let's go find some money!

Boosting Your Income, Part 1: What to Do

I know what you're thinking. You're tired. You already work hard at one job and now I'm expecting you to get another one? No. There are many ways to increase your income that don't involve waiting tables at a pizza joint.

Let's run through a few ideas and maybe you'll get jazzed up about a few. If you decide that, due to family circumstances, you can't possibly spend more time on revenue-producing activities, that's fine. This is about finding what works for you and your situation.

Get a new job

This is what I did and it was a pretty easy decision because I hated my job. I'd been there forever and I knew I was underpaid. I also knew that my job wasn't exactly secure; I might as well have been standing on quicksand. So I had plenty of reasons to be looking for a new job. Fortunately I'd recently passed the CPA exam, so the extra credential made my search a lot easier. I ended up with a 25-percent increase in salary, which helped me tremendously.

Ask for a raise at your current job

Has it been a while since you've had a raise? Have you recently done something that increased revenue or productivity for your company? If you think your job performance warrants an increase, make an appointment with your boss to discuss it. Be prepared to discuss all the reasons why you deserve it.

Sell things you don't use on eBay or Craigslist

This won't bring in a steady income, but if you can pocket a few dollars, that's worth the time you'll spend. Do be careful with Craigslist. I shudder every time I hear about a crime related to that site. Only meet folks in a public place or have others with you if someone needs to come to your home.

Change your living situation

Admittedly this is a big one, but the positive impact on your cash flow can also be big. Glen Craig, who runs the ultra-successful blog FreeFromBroke.com, took this route. He moved in with his parents to get back on track. Here's what he told me about his decision:

> I was struggling with credit card debt. I was finally getting my act together and I was putting a dent in my debt but it was going slowly. As misfortune would have it, I lost my apartment. But I turned the situation into a solution. Rather than look for another place of my own and struggle with what would most likely be higher rent, leaving me less to pay off my credit card debt, I sucked it up and asked my parents if I could move back with them. I knew I needed to really take care of my finances and this was the change that could really turn things around. Thankfully, my parents agreed. With my rent reduced at my parent's, I was able to pour more money into my credit card debt, get it paid off, and build up a nice chunk of savings. It was a hard decision, but it was the right one.

Glen now runs one of the most successful personal finance blogs on the Internet. In fact, it's one of my favorite blogs to read. He traded short-term pain for long-term gain. Obviously, this particular situation won't work for everyone, but it's a good example of how it pays to temporarily give up something.

Another option, if you have a decent-sized home, is to rent out a room to a college student or a retired person.

You'll need to do a good job screening applicants, but if you find a trustworthy tenant, it's a good source of income. And, like Glen's situation, it need only be temporary.

Get a second job

When I was a CPA, I had an office friend who started waitressing at a steakhouse at night to pay off her credit card debt. She'd tried to get a raise, but was turned down. She applied for a personal loan from her own bank, but was denied because her credit score was trashed from late payments on her credit cards.

The tips were awesome and she made a big dent in her debt. She probably would have made more progress if she'd given up her sports car, but she wasn't willing to do that. I can't fault her, though, because she got a second job to pay her bills. I wouldn't be willing to do that, but I do understand that some people really love their cars.

Adjust your tax withholding

Years ago, I used to brag about my tax refund every year. It was often enough to money to head to Panama City or Hilton Head with my pals. As I was getting out of credit card debt and began to get smarter about personal finance, I realized I was giving an interest-free loan to the federal government. I really, really hated the thought of that. I adjusted my withholding amounts with the intent of breaking even or close enough to that. This resulted in a "raise" of about $150 a month. I put this extra amount toward paying off my debt. Your mileage will vary, of course. But

I happen to think that even a $25 monthly boost to your take-home pay is worth it.

Many people enjoy getting the refund because it feels like bonus money. The average refund in 2013 was $2,651. That's a nice chunk of change to get at one time, but think about how much that money could've helped you out during the year. That would have given you another $220.92 per month. That's a lot of cash to add to a minimum monthly payment, don't you think? If you get a nice refund check every year, think about making some changes on your W-4 form so you can have the money now to help pay off your credit card debts.

So how do you do this? Well, if you have an employer, check your W-4 form and change your withholding. When I used this technique to free up money for my debt, I figured out what my taxes would be based on my income and I used a set amount for withholding. It worked like a charm. A couple of warnings, though. If you get a raise during the year, consider the impact on your taxes. You don't want a situation in which you've withheld too little. It's best to withhold a tiny bit more than necessary, just to be safe.

This strategy is often a suggested technique for saving for the holidays. After you pay off your debt, you can save some of this cash in a holiday account for the next year. But for now, it's full-court press on debt!

Refinance your car loan

If you have a steady job and you're not behind on bills, you might be able to negotiate a lower rate with your current lender. But if you've tried it and it didn't work out, consider refinancing your loan at a lower rate elsewhere. You'll increase your cash flow each month because your loan payment will be lower. Getting a lower rate can reduce your monthly payment and then you'll use the extra cash to throw at your credit card debt.

So you have the extra cash for credit card debt, but you'll also pay less on interest while you pay it off. Shop around for the best rates and pay attention to the fine print. Check out LendingTree.com, Bankrate.com, and Credit.com to find current rates and options. You can also check with your local bank and credit unions.

Refinancing with another lender involves transferring the car's title from one lender to another. You may have to pay an early-payment penalty with your current lender, and financing costs with your new lender, so include that in the cost when you make a decision. Do your research so you know what costs are involved and you don't get taken for a ride. (Sorry, I can't resist a good pun, and that was too easy to pass up!)

Negotiate with your credit card company

In Chapter 9, I offer seven strategies to help you boost your credit score. Strategy #6 involves negotiation with your credit card company. In that section, I talk more about the things you can do to specifically raise your score, but some of the ideas also work well for reducing your debt load and thus increasing your cash flow.

Right off the bat, I'll tell you that the first person who answers the phone, the customer service rep, probably can't grant your wish. But be very polite and ask to speak with that person's manager. If you get pushback, say goodbye and call again 10 minutes later to get a different rep. By pushback, I mean the rep claims he or she can't help you.

Here are some areas in which you may have room to negotiate:

Ask for a lower interest rate. Only do this if you have a good record as a customer. It's possible to be in debt and still be making your credit card payments on time. If you still have a good credit score, you might be able to get a lower interest rate. A lower interest rate means less interest expense you'll have to pay over time. It doesn't lower your minimum payment much, if at all, but you do save money over the time it takes you to pay off the debt.

Collect any offers you've received in the mail. There's a lot of competition out there for good customers, especially if you are in debt but still pay on time. This is because the credit card company makes money off the interest you pay. And because you pay your bills on time, the lender likely won't have to write off your debt. If your current credit card has a 15% APR and you have an offer for a 12% APR card, then let your issuer know that you're a hot commodity. Tell the customer service rep about your new offer. Of course, you'll say that you want to be loyal to your current issuer and feel you've been a good customer. (Warning: I've seen this backfire. During the recent recession I was often told by readers that their interest rate went up instead of down when they attempted this. So proceed with your eyes wide open—and with a great payment history in your pocket.)

Don't wing it. Before you make the call have a script ready. Practice it until you sound sincere and there's not a hint of desperation in your voice. Your goal is to sound as though you're making a request because you deserve it.

Consider a balance transfer

I've written about balance transfers so many times, I've lost count. The reason I write it about it so much, though, is because I get so many e-mails asking me if this is a good option. In many cases, it is. It's an awesome way to save on interest while paying down debt. And a transfer helps you pay it off faster, too. But it can get a little complicated if you aren't familiar with how transfers work.

Here's an example of how it works: Let's say you have a $10,000 balance on credit card A and it has an 18% APR. You get approved for a balance transfer credit card, which we'll cleverly dub credit card B, that offers a 0% introductory rate. These kinds of introductory rates usually last anywhere from six to 18 months.

So you transfer the $10,000 balance on credit card A to credit card B, your new balance transfer card. And guess what? If you pay attention to the details, you get to pay off your debt while paying zero interest for the introductory period. What do I mean by paying attention to the details? Balance transfers can be a thing of beauty, but they can also come back to bite you if you don't know what you're doing. Be sure you keep in mind that the details will vary by issuer, so read the fine print to be aware of the specifics for your particular card.

Over the years I've seen the most common mistakes people make, so I give you my seven secrets for a successful balance transfer:

Secret #1: Know the deadline for the balance transfer offer. Usually, you'll have a certain amount of time to make the request, such as 30 days or three months. There's no need to dilly-dally around with this. Seriously, if you've gone to the trouble to get approved for a balance transfer, go ahead and do it as quickly as possible. Don't waste a minute getting yourself in position to save money and get out of debt. The deadline will be noted in the Schumer box, right where the length of time is listed. By the way, the Schumer box is an actual box on the terms and conditions that displays all the rates and fees for a credit card.

Secret #2: Don't forget to make monthly payments during the introductory period. I've seen it all when it comes to balance transfer mistakes, so I must include this one. And to be fair, the credit card companies don't make it easy to digest all the rules. So just in case you thought this card was like a "get out of jail free card," a la Monopoly, it's not. In this game, there's no free lunch. This is like any other balance that you owe, and you have to make monthly payments or you could end up in a bad place. This leads us right into Secret #3.

Secret #3: Make your payments on time or you could lose the introductory rate. You have to read the your credit card agreement's fine print to know the circumstances that could cause you to lose your 0% introductory rate. Sometimes the terms are really strict, and if you make a payment that's just one day late, you could lose your introductory rate. Tough love! In other cases, you don't lose your introductory rate unless you're more than 60 days late, but at that point, you'd lose the introductory rate and maybe even get stuck with a 30% penalty interest rate. That would be awful, right?

Your mantra: *Do whatever it takes to pay your bill on time.*

These days, there's so much technology to keep your brain in working order, there's just no excuse for forgetting something as crucial as a timely payment. Set calendar reminders on your iPhone, set up automatic payments from your checking account, or sign up for text or e-mail reminders from the credit card company.

Secret #4: Know when the 0% introductory rate ends. You'll see this information in the "terms and conditions" of your new card. Lately I've been seeing 0% introductory rates that last for up to 18 months, which is pretty darn good. Every once in a while the issuers will go a little nuts and offer a 24-month deal, but I haven't seen that in a while. Your goal with this card is to pay off your balance during the interest-free period, if at all possible. If the amount is too high to eliminate completely during the introductory period, don't sweat it. Just paying off a chunk is a nice start, and you'll still save on interest.

Now, before we calculate your monthly payment, you should know that you'll probably pay a balance transfer fee. This fee ranges from 3 to 5% of the total amount transferred. Occasionally, a few cards boast 0% introductory APRs with no transfer fees. As of this writing the Chase Slate credit card is the only one I'm aware of that waives the fee if you complete the transfer within 60 days of opening an account. I keep waiting for them to take this perk away, but I'm impressed that they've stuck with it for as long as they have.

For our purposes, let's assume there's a 3% transfer fee. With $10,000, you'd pay $300 (10,000 x .03). So the total amount you'll have pay off is $10,300. It's a pain to pay the fee, for sure. But keep in mind how much you're saving by not paying interest. In many cases, it's well worth paying the transfer fee to get out from under an oppressively high APR for a year or more.

So if you have an 18-month 0% introductory period, divide your balance by 18:

$$10,300 / 18 = \$572.22$$

That's the amount you need to pay each month in order to pay off the debt during the interest-free period. And remember: if you can't pay that much, just pick an amount you can afford and pay down a decent chunk of your debt. Once you make a commitment to an amount, stick with it unless you have a dire financial emergency.

I suggest checking your progress every few months just to keep yourself psyched up. This is also a good way to make sure you've stuck with your plan. Which leads me to the next secret.

Secret #5: Stick with your payoff plan. Remember how you figured out how much you have to pay each month to pay off your debt? Embrace it. Enjoy making the payments. And don't deviate from the plan. You can't take a month off from the plan and use that money for a beach weekend or a fishing trip. As I mentioned, if you don't pay off your balance during the introductory period, you'll have to start paying interest on it at the go-to rate.

Secret #6: Make payments on your old card until you're sure the transfer is complete. You can't suddenly stop making payments to your old issuer, because it takes a little time for the transfer to go through. It can take weeks for a balance transfer to complete, so keep making payments on your old credit card until you get the "all clear" from both banks. To confirm the transfer is complete, check your account online and look for a balance of zero. I'd also call the issuer and ask for verbal confirmation.

Here's why I'm making a big deal out of this. If you stop making payments before the balance transfer has been completed, you could miss a payment. This means you'll be hit with a late payment fee; if this goes on long enough, it can hurt your credit score if your late payment gets reported to the credit bureaus. This is one of those sneaky little things that can sabotage your efforts to clean up your credit while trying to get out of debt.

Secret #7: Don't make new purchases with your balance transfer card. There are two issues here that trip people up. First, if you continue to make new purchases, you won't get out of debt. Remember how we calculated the amount you needed to pay every month to get out of debt during your interest-free introductory period? Don't screw that up with new purchases. Put away the credit cards while you're in debt. You've already agreed (twice!) that you'll stop using credit cards, anyway.

Second, don't assume new purchases are covered by the 0% introductory rate. You'd have to have a balance transfer card that also offered a 0% APR introductory rate on *purchases*. If that isn't part of the terms for your balance transfer card, then your new purchases are subject to the purchase APR, which is also usually the go-to rate for any remaining balance left on your card after the introductory period expires.

So if you have a variable 14.99% APR on purchases, those new golf clubs or designer duds will accrue interest at that rate once the grace period ends. The grace period is the time between your purchase and the due date. Sure, you can avoid the interest if you pay the amount in full during the grace period, but why spend that money? Use the money to pay off your debt instead. Use your old clubs or get some affordable clothes at Old Navy or Target in the meantime. Treat yourself later when you have the money and it's part of your overall budget plan.

Balance transfer cards for those who don't have excellent FICO scores

If you have a score around or a little below 700, you still might qualify for a balance transfer card that offers a lower rate than the one you currently have, so it's worth checking into. For example, at the time I wrote this book, Capital One's QuicksilverOne Cash Rewards Credit Card, which targets those with average credit, was offering a balance transfer at 22.9% APR. I know that sounds a little hideous, but if you're paying 25.99% on your current card, this might help a little bit. Of course, you have to think about the transfer fee, but in the case of the QuicksilverOne, the fee is waived.

Anyway, the point is, do some research when you're ready to proceed. The economy changes and this can alter the terms of the credit card at any point in time. Maybe you'll get lucky at just the right time and find a good balance transfer deal.

Boosting Your Income, Part 2: What Not to Do

I encourage you to avoid these strategies. It's possible they could work and probably have worked for others. But the risks are high. Honestly, I've seen folks really get into worse shape using these strategies.

Don't use a home equity line of credit

Before the Great Recession, times were good if you owned a home. It wasn't unusual for people to do one of these two things if they needed more cash to spend: get a home equity line of credit, or HELOC; or get a home equity loan. If you were one of those involved in these financial tactics, you may have gotten burned when the real estate market crashed. This is how a lot of folks ended up underwater with their mortgages (*underwater* meaning that the home is worth less than they owe).

Here's a simple equation for figuring out how much equity you have:

Your home's worth: $200,000

You owe: $150,000

Your equity: $50,000, or 25% of $200,000; this is a 75% loan-to-value ratio

You also need to have good credit and an income to get approved for a HELOC.

What's the difference?

A HELOC is essentially a second mortgage; just the thought of it makes my throat close up a little. You use your home as collateral for another loan. The risk? If you can't pay your new debt, you might lose your home. With a HELOC, you get a credit line and you borrow what you need. You make payments only on what you borrow, not on the entire credit line. In this regard, it works similarly to a credit card.

A home equity loan is very different. With this loan, you borrow against the value of your home. You then receive a lump sum of cash which you repay over time with a fixed payment. The standards were recently raised; lenders now want you to have an 80% loan-to-value ratio or less. In the previous example, you'd probably qualify for a loan because your loan-to-value ratio is 75%. Using this method basically means you are risking your home to pay off your credit card bills. This was a smarter bet years ago than it is right now, but I'm talking about it because I know a few of you will still consider it, especially if you can save money by eliminating a chunk of interest. Plus, many people like the tax deduction they receive because it's a type of mortgage.

Here's the danger: *Unless you're a model of self-discipline, you might start using the credit cards again.* Then what you'd have is a home equity loan to pay plus *more* credit card debt. Yes, this is serious business, and I suggest you make this a last resort. And even then, it's still probably a bad idea.

Don't use an emergency fund

Credit card debt is toxic debt, so it's important to get rid of it as quickly as you can. But you don't want to use your emergency fund if doing so wipes it out. You need a safety net while you get out of debt. I can't stress this enough.

Here's a rule of thumb: If you have a fund that's less than $2,500, don't use this money to pay off your debt. If, however, you have $4,000 in an emergency fund, then consider applying $1,500—the amount you have in excess of that $2,500—to your credit card debt. You're welcome to adjust this formula based on your needs. If you're single, you may be able to take more of a risk. If you have three children, you'll want to be especially careful about having a healthy rainy-day fund.

Don't withdraw from your 401K

One of the highlights of my blogging year was a guest post by Jean Chatzky, best-selling author and the financial editor for NBC's *Today Show*. She addressed this very issue. Basically she advises not to do this, mostly because it's risky:

First of all, not every 401K program allows you to borrow. If you are allowed to borrow from your 401K, then you pay it back with interest through payroll deductions. If you decided to leave your job or you happen to lose your job, you may be expected to pay it back quickly. If you don't pay it back, the IRS considers it a distribution and you'll pay a 10-percent penalty on top of taxes on the distribution.

So think about how terrible it would be if you lost your job and you couldn't pay it back. Just don't raid your 401K if you can help it. This is one of those things that should be off limits unless you're avoiding something drastic, like bankruptcy. Once you start treating your 401K like a piggy bank, you're liable to lean on it again. Your 401K is a wealth-building tool, so treat it as though it's untouchable.

6

Create Your Debt Escape Plan

Now that you have your budget all set and you know how much money you can throw at your debt, it's time to decide how to proceed. This is where your money personality and your learning style come in to play.

Before we hop into the nuts and bolts of your debt escape, I want to give you a friendly reminder. No, I'm not going to tell you (for the third time) that you can't use credit cards while you're getting out of debt. I just want to remind you that the success of your plan hinges on one little practice: *Make mindful spending a habit.*

You may have heard of the concept of mindful spending. If not, don't worry. I'm not going to get all Zen on you. When I talk about mindful spending, it simply means that when you spend even a dime, you're thinking about what you're getting in return for that dime. It's not just that you're paying attention whenever you hand over your money (which you should be), but that you're thinking about whether this is how you really want to spend that money. Are you getting something you want or need in return?

When you put together your budget, you had to think about how you spend your money. You have your blueprint for financial success; all you need to do now is make sure you follow that plan. You follow your plan by setting up a system to track your spending. This forces you to engage in mindful spending because you look at the actual numbers.

You might look at last month's clothing bill and wonder why you bought ballet flats when you already had a pair in a similar color. When you practice mindful spending, you think it through *before* the purchase, not after. Even if you stay within your budget, you've blown that money on flats that you don't really need. You could have bought something else, or spent it on a birthday gift for a friend. See where I'm going with this? Mindful spending not only helps you stay on budget, but it also enhances your life because you're spending money on things that matter to you.

One thing that often knocks people off track are impulse buys. But once you get into the habit of mindful spending, you automatically start thinking about each purchase in a different way. Okay, that's my lecture on mindful spending. Now, hopefully you're ready to put the structure in place.

Organizing Your Credit Card Debt for Payoff

Let me say up-front that there's no correct way to pay off debt, contrary to what you hear in the media. The objective here is to put yourself in the best position possible for success. If the method you choose works, it's the correct way for you. You're in an emotional state when you're in debt, so sometimes the most "logical" method just doesn't motivate you. And just because your pal's method worked for her doesn't mean it will work for you. This is why you took the Money Personality Quiz in Chapter 3. This is valuable information to have as you make decisions about how to proceed. What you know about your learning style will help, too.

There are two tried-and-true methods to pay off debt, plus one newer one that yours truly invented. We'll look at each one in turn, and I'll make a note of the personality types that might be a good match for each. We'll cover the Debt Avalanche, the Debt Snowball, and—my own personal creation—the Debt Blizzard. At first, I called it the Debt Flurry, but that didn't sound fierce enough. As you can see, I decided to stick with snow-related terms just to keep everything consistent.

No matter what plan you choose, make sure you stick with it or you'll end up with a Debt Glacier—that is, a ginormous debt that hangs around forever because it's so slow moving.

Create a Debt Avalanche

The Debt Avalanche method is sometimes called the Debt Stacking method, but I don't think that's a good name for it. With Debt Stacking, you may stack your debt in any order you please, but with the Avalanche method, you start with the highest interest rate first. You've already listed your credit card debts on the worksheet, right? All you have to do is get the correct order by interest rate.

Here's an example of how to order your debts for the avalanche treatment:

CREDIT CARD DEBT WORKSHEET: AVALANCHE

Credit Card	Balance	Interest Rate (APR)	Mininum Payment
Capital One	$7,000.00	22%	$198.33
Chase	$2,500.00	16%	$58.33
Discover	$1,500.00	14%	$32.50
Wells Fargo	$3,000.00	11%	$57.50

Best personality type: The Money Master, of course. The Money Master would not be happy with any method that didn't save the most money. Also, the Clever Cheapskate and the Terrified Tightwad might appreciate the logic and money-saving approach in this method. You do save the most money, but you need to be disciplined because you don't get that quick boost from paying off a debt.

Throw a Debt Snowball

This method is advocated by a few personal finance gurus. The success of this method relies on the idea that paying off your smallest balance first will give you a big psychological boost. That boost, in turn, gives you momentum to stay motivated and continue paying off your debt.

After you pay the smallest debt, you then set your sights on the next smallest debt. Interest rates are ignored with this method, so you will pay more in interest expenses. That's why this method is often criticized by anyone who can operate a calculator. But remember what I said about logic? I'm not saying throw it out the window, but you have to know yourself and go with what motivates you.

CREDIT CARD DEBT WORKSHEET: SNOWBALL

Credit Card	Balance	Interest Rate (APR)	Minimum Payment
Discover	$1,500.00	14%	$32.50
Chase	$2,500.00	16%	$58.33
Wells Fargo	$3,000.00	11%	$57.50
CapitalOne	$7,000.00	22%	$198.33

See how this changes everything? You end up paying a lot of interest on the CapitalOne card, but you get to pay off more of your debts along the way. So if the number of debts has you up at night, and you're fine with spending more to take that approach, who am I to argue with that? I just want you to be aware that you're paying more this way.

Best personality type: The Budget Buster tends to make emotional decisions, and this method gives a quick psychological boost. This is also a good one for the Unconcerned Consumer. Getting quick wins along the way might actually keep this type motivated.

Go all out with a Debt Blizzard

What happens when you throw a snowball at an avalanche? You get a little blizzard effect from the impact. At least, I think you do! The Debt Blizzard combines the best aspects of the Debt Snowball and the Debt Avalanche methods. This is for those who want a quick fix, but who would also rather save on interest expense in the long run.

A group of professors from prestigious universities, including Duke and Washington University in St. Louis, published research about the psychology of debt management in a 2011 issue of the *Journal of Marketing*. They talk about "debt account aversion," which refers to the consumer's tendency to pay off the smallest debt first instead of the debt with the highest interest rate, which the authors aren't thrilled about it. In fact, they say that "debt account aversion might enable consumers to win the battle but lose the war." Well, with the Debt Blizzard, you can win a battle and then go back and win the whole dang war.

CREDIT CARD DEBT WORKSHEET: BLIZZARD

Credit Card	Balance	Interest Rate (APR)	Minimum Payment
Discover	$1,500.00	14%	$32.50
Capital One	$7,000.00	22%	$198.33
Chase	$2,500.00	16%	$58.33
Wells Fargo	$3,000.00	11%	$57.50

Best personality type: The Budget Buster, the Clever Cheapskate, and the Unconcerned Consumer might find this approach helpful. I don't see the Money Master or the Terrified Tightwad enjoying this method because they're more into saving the most money possible rather needing a quick boost to stay motivated. They're already motivated to pay off debt.

Choose Your Target Debt

Remember the credit card worksheet you put together in Chapter 4? You're going to use that to arrange your debts in the order in which you want to pay them off. For example, if you choose the Debt Avalanche, you'll start with the debt with the highest interest rate. And remember the $220 debt-escape money you found in chapters 4 and 5? That's the additional amount you'll throw at the minimum payment. Looking at the sample Debt Avalanche method:

- **Target debt:** Capital One, $7,000 balance, 22% APR
- **Minimum payment:** $198.33
- **Extra money found:** $220
- **New monthly payment:** $418.33
- **Payoff period:** 21 months

I used the payoff calculator on Bankrate.com to determine the payoff period. So if this were your debt, and you started paying the extra amount in April 2015, you'd be free from this debt in December 2016.

During this time you'd pay only the minimum amounts on your other debts. This shows why some folks like the Snowball method or might want to try my Blizzard approach. Just over two years is a long time to wait to wipe out a debt. This is why I suggest the Blizzard method: Get a quick emotional lift by wiping out your smallest debt first, and *then* tackle the debt with the highest interest rate.

However, if saving money motivates you, then you'll find a way to stay energized about sticking to your plan even if the target debt is huge.

Calculate Your Target Month

I don't believe in picking a specific date early on because that sets people up for failure. Things will go wrong and you will have money emergencies or at least financial speed bumps along the way. It's best to pick the target month so that you don't risk getting demoralized. But as you get a little closer to your target month, you'll be in a position to estimate a more exact date.

In the previous example, you'll be free from your first debt ($7,000) in 25 months. Then you move to the second debt, which is the $2,500 debt if you're using the Avalanche method, and add the $220 to the monthly payment. See how this works? You can use the calculator on CreditCards.com to determine how long it will take you to wipe out your credit card debts.

Ways to Keep Track of Your Budget

If you already have a budget and it just hasn't worked for you or it's outdated, you might be comfortable going directly into personal finance software or using a money management site. There are three possible approaches to consider when it comes to automated financial help. You can use online money management software, use personal finance software applications, or create your own budget software in Excel.

But what if you've never had a budget or you aren't comfortable using an automated method for budgeting? No problem. For some of you, the good old-fashioned envelope method might be just what the doctor ordered. Warning: Exceptional envelope-stuffing skills are needed.

The Cash Envelope method

I know several people who have used the original envelopes method of budgeting, and it really helped them get a handle on their spending. I also know people who use this method on an ongoing basis. If you decide that you need to stop using credit cards altogether, this is a method to consider.

Here's how it works: You label an envelope for each expense and for sources of income. You take your income and place the appropriate amount into the labeled envelope. You pay your bills using the cash for each expense. When the envelope is empty, you stop spending in that category. For example, let's say you allocate $400 to spend on groceries this month. Each week, you take $100 to the grocery store with you. But when your grocery envelope is empty, you're done spending on groceries for the month, even if it's not the end of the month. You eat whatever is in the pantry or the freezer at that point.

Obviously, you need to count your cash every few days or at least weekly to make sure you have enough to make it through the month. A quick tip is to keep a running total of what's left in each envelope on a sticky note pasted on the envelope. If you write it on the envelope itself, you'd have to use a new set of envelopes every month. You have better things to do with your time.

At the end of the month, the remaining cash goes into a savings account, an emergency fund, or both.

A few twists on the Cash Envelope method

The traditional Cash Envelope method might not be the best solution for someone who has a fairly high income, because you should be investing that extra cash and not have it sitting around in a bunch of envelopes. And yes, you can have credit card debt and have a high income; it happens all the time!

If you're a high earner, you can take a hybrid approach to this method and make regular contributions to your retirement or mutual fund accounts while using the envelopes for everyday spending. This just goes to prove what I've been saying all along: There's not a magic method that works for everyone. And it's perfectly acceptable to take a well-known method and bend it to your own needs.

Here's another twist to try: If a specific spending category has proven problematic for you, use the Cash Envelope method as a temporary measure to establish self-discipline in that area. For instance, when I get busy, my biggest weakness is eating out. My youngest just left for college, but I assure you they always come back home and call when they need things. So I still consider myself a working mom! I'm tired at the end of the day, especially if I have a book deadline. Ironically, it was a huge problem I had to get control of while writing this book about getting out of debt.

If I hadn't gotten it under control when I did, I would have set up an envelope that contained the cash allotted for eating out. Then, when it was empty, I would have resorted to my old standby of peanut-butter-and-jelly sandwiches.

- **Pros:** It's a simple way to assess your spending and make positive changes. You don't have to worry about categorizing expenses in a software program and there's a zero learning curve. Some folks use this method to get a grip on things and then move on to an automated budget.

- **Cons:** Carrying around loads of cash isn't a safe thing to do, so you'll need to plan for expensive items and have the cash available at the right time. You also don't have a cash flow history that you can easily view. It's really quite motivating to look at charts and patterns and see your debt go down and your savings go up at some point.

   And what about inflation? Prices change and you need to think about that. This method requires attention to detail and the ability to make adjustments when costs increase.

- **Personality types:** Anyone who tends to overspend, especially the Budget Buster. Also, the Unconcerned

Consumer might find this a good way to ease into the concept of a budget.

- **Learning styles:** Kinesthetic, because you can touch the money, and that helps you "internalize" your budget. You also have hands-on control over the money. I think we all enjoy that feeling to a degree. There's a payoff here for the visual person, too, as you can see the results of your budgeting. All good things.

To DIY or Not to DIY?

Should you create your own budget worksheet? Any of the personality types might have an interest in this. If your learning style is Kinesthetic, you might enjoy this approach as long as you have the technical skills to pull it off. All you need is a sound knowledge of Excel and you can go to town churning out a custom budgeting worksheet for yourself or for your entire family.

If you want to go old school and write it on a ledger you buy at Staples, that's fine, too. I don't recommend this approach for Visuals unless you use colored markers and things like that. You're liable to get bored and lose interest without an interesting interface to work with.

The downside of the DIY approach is that you won't have the ability to track and categorize expenses the way so many of the advanced programs do. But if you're an Excel wizard, you might be up to whipping out a whole slew of worksheets to help you manage your money. Even if you have the skills, it's a lot of work. And I want things to be easy for you so you stick with it.

- **Pros:** Total control, baby! You can customize to your heart's content and get that rush when the columns add up just the way you want them to. Plus, you don't have to deal with ads on Websites. That's a benefit, for sure.

- **Cons:** It's a lot of work to get this set up. But if you enjoy creating Excel worksheets, then you probably won't think of it as work. You still won't get all the bells and whistles that come with a Website or packaged software—well, unless you're an Excel god or goddess.

- **Personality types:** Any type can do this, except for maybe the Unconcerned Consumer—because, you know, they wouldn't have any interest in creating their own money-management system when they aren't concerned about their money.

- **Learning styles:** Kinesthetic folks usually enjoy this type of hands-on stuff, but you can customize it take advantage of how you prefer to interact with software.

Personal-Finance Software vs. Free Money-Management Websites

Okay, here's the scoop. With personal finance software, you buy the program either online or in stores. Then you install it on your personal computer or laptop. Here are some examples in this category: Microsoft Money, AceMoney, and Intuit's Quicken Starter. If you're concerned about privacy and security, this is a good option for you.

You have to be very diligent about computer backups because the information is living on your computer, not on the Internet. I want to point this out just in case you don't have an automatic backup procedure already in place. I use Dropbox and it's worked out well for me.

Free money-management Websites store your financial data online. The service is free, but you'll encounter ads and marketing suggestions. It can be annoying, but if you like the interface, you'll learn to ignore the credit card suggestions or whatever pops up in your e-mail or on the screen.

The biggest concern most people have when they think about entering their account information online is whether or not it's secure. You'll want to check out the specific procedures for each site, but generally, these sites have solid protections in place. For instance, Mint uses servers that contain the information in a separate unmarked building. There are other layers of security in place such as a required palm read to enter the building. Sounds like a James Bond movie script, doesn't it?

Having said all this, nothing is totally safe. Everything has some risk. I'm just saying that I'm willing to take a little risk to make budgeting my money easier and even fun to do. If that statement makes it sound like I use Mint, well, I do. I want to get that out there before you read my review. I do love it and I can't even pretend to be unbiased. But I don't have a financial relationship with them, so I do not benefit at all if you decide to use them. Mint simply works well with my money personality, the Money Master (and former Unconcerned Consumer), and is complemented by a Visual learning style.

Here are some examples in this category: Mint.com, Quicken Online, and Cashbox. There are others might be better for you, and we'll get to those in a minute.

Personal-finance software applications

First, let's look at a few examples of personal finance applications. Some require that you enter all your transactions manually. For those starting out, I actually recommend this. There's nothing like getting down and dirty with your numbers. The first one seems to be very popular, according to my readers, and it requires a hands-on approach. Note that pricing was accurate as of this writing, but may have changed since that time.

You Need a Budget (YNAB)

I really like the way this budget looks. It's clean and colorful, but there's also a lot of white space, which makes it easy on the eyes. The approach is just right for someone who doesn't have a lot of budgeting experience. You do, however, have to enter your own transactions so you'll need to be disciplined.

- **Cost:** $60

- **Pros:** It's a user-friendly design and a good fit for those who aren't tech savvy. They offer classes to get you started off on the right foot and I think that's awesome. There are also mobile apps you can use.

- **Cons:** This software doesn't cover investments and other more complicated factors.

- **Personality type:** The Terrified Tightwad, as this doesn't require handing over sensitive financial data. The Budget Buster and the Unconcerned Consumer could also benefit from this simple budget approach.

- **Learning style:** It's a great choice for Visuals, but I think any learning type can find a way to make this program work for their style. Kinesthetic learners will enjoy the process of entering their own data and seeing the budget take shape.

- **System requirements:** Windows XP, Vista 7 or 8; Apple Mac OS X Snow Leopard 10.6 through Mavericks 10.9

- **Apps:** Android, iPhone, Kindle Fire

- **Website:** *www.youneedabudget.com*

AceMoney

This application takes an all-inclusive approach to personal finance. It offers a variety of financial calculators, which I think is cool, as I'm a money geek. This is for people who are serious about their finances and about setting goals. You can sync up multiple accounts and track spending that way.

Cost: Regularly $49.99, but on the home page it was being offered for $34.99 at the time of writing. There's an AceMoney Lite version that's free. It's still a good program, but you're limited to only two accounts. Here's the Website for the free version: *www.mechcad.net/products/acemoney/ free-personal-finance-software-quicken-alternative.shtml.*

- **Pros:** Constantly updates stock prices so your account values (for example, 401Ks and stock options) are up to date; monitors spending habits; handles finances in multiple currencies; has many budget categories to choose from, but you can also create your own account types.

- **Cons:** It's a straightforward design and somewhat businesslike compared to other programs I've seen, but some of you may actually prefer that; no phone apps are available at this time.

- **Personality type:** The Money Master will love this because AceMoney is for those who want great tools to help them manage their money. The Clever Cheapskate might also enjoy the powerful features of this program.

- **Learning style:** It's not the best choice for Visual learners. The other types—Auditory, Kinesthetic, and Read/Write—will find this program more compatible with their styles.

- **System requirements:** Windows, Mac OS X, Linux

- **Apps:** None at the time of this writing, but they say they're working on apps for Android and iPhone/iPad

- **Website:** *http://store.hermanstreet.com/business-office/acemoney-download/?&ICID=pin-acemoney%202013-6-12pf*

Intuit's Quicken Starter

This application isn't as full of features as AceMoney or some other programs, but it's a good way to get started on budgeting. I think the design is appealing (see, there's my Visual learner bias showing!), and the program is pretty user friendly. This program helps you track progress against your goals. You can sync your account information to this program, too, so you don't have to physically enter your transactions.

Previous versions had an issue with rolling over leftover money to the next month. For instance, say you budgeted $500 for groceries and only spent $475. The $25 would have gotten lost. But new versions have supposedly fixed that bug.

- **Cost:** Regularly $39.99, but on the home page it was being offered for $29.99 at the time of writing.

- **Pros:** Categorizes every transaction, and the data can be viewed in graphs or charts; there's a free mobile app; Quicken sends a text alert if there are unusual changes in your activity; you can import data into TurboTax.

- **Cons:** It doesn't offer investment features, so if you want a one-stop financial planning program, this isn't for you.

- **Personality type:** The Budget Buster and the Unconcerned Consumer could benefit from this program. The Clever Cheapskate usually has investments, so this is an unlikely match. Same with the Money Master, who loves a more powerful program.

- **Learning style:** It's a good choice for visual learners.
- **System requirements:** Windows XP SP3+, Vista SP1 and Windows 7/8 (32- and 64-bit)
- **Apps:** Android mobile or tablet, iPhone, iPad, iPad Touch; not compatible at this time with Windows Phone or BlackBerry
- **Website:** *http://quicken.intuit.com/?cid=int_qkn_aff_cj_3475222&priorityCode=1275500000&PID=3475222&source=cj_pfm*

Moneydance

May I just say that I love the name? This really makes personal finance sound more like a graceful waltz than a head-banging activity. It conjures up a nice mental image.

With this program you can connect your banking and account information. It even offers bill pay, but not all banks support this feature when it's attached to an application-based system.

- **Cost:** $49.99
- **Pros:** Makes it easy to set up budgets; shows you if you're over or under budget; categorizes the transactions downloaded from your bank; handles multiple currencies.
- **Cons:** Not quite as visually appealing as some of the other programs. It also doesn't seem as user-friendly, but unless you're a technophobe, it's unlikely to be a real issue.

- **Personality type:** The Clever Cheapskate and the Money Master are both candidates for this program. The Budget Buster and the Unconcerned Consumer need a more straightforward approach than this program offers.

- **Learning style:** It's not the best choice for Visual learners. The other styles should do fine with Moneydance.

- **System requirements:** Windows, Mac, and Linux

- **Apps:** Available for free for iPhone, iPad, iPad Touch; recently became available for Android

- **Website:** *http://moneydance.com*

Free Money-Management Websites

Note that these are free. If you decide to go the personal-finance software route and pay for a package, that's different. You pay one time and then it's yours; in some cases, you even get free updates. But to me, taking on a recurring monthly fee to manage your money doesn't make sense. There's no need to add another expense while you're working to get out of debt. In fact, I'd say the last thing you need right now is a new monthly expense. So let's do this budgeting thing for free. And I'm going for simple so that you stay focused on your goal: getting out of credit card debt.

Yes, there are all kinds of special rankings or scores or credit health checks you can get with premium versions, but all that stuff can get distracting. Long live the KISS approach to budgeting.

Mint

With Mint, you do have to link to your bank accounts, but as I already mentioned, their security is pretty tight. If you're willing to link to your accounts, you get up-to-date and in-depth analysis of your financial data.

There are a lot of reasons I like Mint. You can set up a budget, set retirement goals, create payoff plans, and more. I love the graphics, especially. Mint tracks your spending, and you can view your finances in pie charts, graphs, and bar charts. You can compare your spending month-to-month and year-to-year. I think it's very helpful to view your spending history because it helps you understand your patterns.

- **Pros:** Easy to use and getting started is a breeze; you can set up categories and get e-mail notices when you're approaching budget limits; easy to personalize Mint so you can use it the way that works for you.

- **Cons:** You'll see ads and suggestions for financial products; you just have to ignore them.

- **Apps:** iPhone, iPad, Android, Android tablets, Windows 8, and Windows 8 phones

- **Personality type:** Mint should appeal to all of the money personality types, except for the Terrified Tightwad because this requires handing over sensitive financial data.

- **Learning style:** Definitely a great choice for Visual learners! But because there are so many features and so many ways to use Mint, I think any learning type can find a way to make this program work for his or her style.

- **Website:** *www.mint.com*

Budgetpulse

If you don't feel comfortable handing over details of your financial accounts, Budgetpulse is worth a look. This is also a good choice for someone who's just getting his or her budgeting sea legs.

You can set up a budget and analyze your net worth, among other things. I do like the goals feature. You can have private goals if you prefer, or you can decide to make your goals public and share them with others on the site.

- **Pros:** Simple to use; the interface isn't technical, and the Website does a good job of explaining how everything works; not a lot of bells and whistles with Budgetpulse, but it gets the job done.

- **Cons:** You have to enter your own transaction information (or download it from files) because it isn't connected to your accounts. Be sure you're willing to do this or using Budgetpulse won't work for you.

- **Apps:** At the time of this writing it didn't have a mobile app.

- **Personality type:** Any personality type who isn't comfortable with having financial account information on the Internet, such as the Terrified Tightwad. Also, the Budget Buster and the Unconcerned Consumer might benefit from the hands-on approach used here. It's also easy for beginning budgeters to get used to, and that's a plus for all of the money personality types.

- **Learning styles:** Kinesthetic and Read/Write styles, but really, any learning style could adjust to this simple approach. The Read/Write and Auditory styles would enjoy the forum aspect of this site.

- **Website:** *www.budgetpulse.com*

BudgetTracker

This Website is pretty flexible. You can link to your online bank accounts or you can choose not to. There's also a premium (read: pricier) version that offers unlimited accounts.

- **Pros:** It has some handy tools, such as forecasting and calendar reminders; good choice for those who have security concerns.

- **Cons:** You have to enter your own transaction information (or download it from files) because it isn't connected to your accounts.

- **Apps:** Android, iPhone, iPad

- **Personality type:** The Terrified Tightwad would appreciate the flexibility of not having to link accounts. Also, the Budget Buster and the Unconcerned Consumer might benefit from the direct approach used here.

- **Learning styles:** Kinesthetic and Read/Write styles, but really, any learning style could adjust to this simple approach. It's not a very pretty interface, which might turn off those who favor a visual approach to their finances.

- **Website:** *www.budgettracker.com*

7

Staying Motivated When Things Go Wrong

I'm an optimistic person by nature, but I'm also a realist. Yes, you can be both. I'm optimistic that I'll get what I want, but I'm realistic enough to know that something will go wrong along the way. And things *will* go wrong because that's just the way life is. I want to share some thoughts with you about staying positive. You need to try to stay positive from this point or you'll approach the strategies in this chapter with the wrong mind-set. Believe it or not, you can turn optimism into a habit.

Keep It Positive

The trick is setting yourself up for success so that you keep going no matter what roadblocks you encounter. The longer you stick with your debt escape plan, the more confidence you'll have that you can solve problems as they arise. I realize, of course, that it's not always easy.

When I was working on my own escape from debt, I heard through the grapevine at work that my position wasn't what you'd call, well, chiseled in stone. I had two problems: shaky job security, and a mountain of debt I was still paying off. You know what? I hated my life during that time. But I eventually saw it as an opportunity. I started looking for a job as if my life depended on it. I ended up with a more interesting job at a much better company. Oh, and my income increased by 25 percent. I threw the extra cash at my debt. This was huge for me.

The process of getting out of debt brings on a whirlwind of emotions. If you haven't experienced it, you can't really understand what it feels like. One day, you feel optimistic and you tell yourself, *I've got this!* And the next day, you're thinking, *I'm a loser. How did I let this happen?* All of these emotions are very normal. So let yourself off the hook right now for thinking you should be tough enough to control your emotions while you go through this. You're plenty tough; if not, you wouldn't still be reading this book!

Now, I do want to say that if you find yourself in a serious depression, please get counseling. There's no shame in that. In fact, I think it takes courage and self-awareness to know when to ask for help. If you feel as though you can't face another day, then talk to someone. My suggestions here are for those who feel okay about the future for the most part, but are feeling temporarily out of whack.

Following is a list of several emotions. Pick the one that applies to you currently and check out the antidotes for it. And you know what? I'd love to hear from you if you try out some of these strategies. If you come up with your own ideas, send me an email and tell me about it.

You're tired of sacrificing

At first you didn't mind. You could see the value in your decision, and it was exciting to apply the saved money to your debt. But for heaven's sake, you need a treat of some kind! Hey, I get it. We're all human, and there's got to be a carrot out there to keep us going sometimes. Try to think of small ways you can treat yourself that don't involve giving in to the expenditures you temporarily gave up.

Mini-treat therapy. Here's a common scenario I hear about all the time: You've given up your weekly dinner and a movie with your partner. Instead, you and your significant other are grilling burgers at home and renting a movie from Redbox. Savings: about $125 for dinner and $23 for tickets. Hmmm...$125 for dinner for two? Yes, you have a thing for fine wine and you can't help yourself when you're out at a nice restaurant. This is why it's important not to give in if you can help it. You might promise yourself you'll drink water and not spend more than necessary, but will you? Really?

That's why it's better to try and do a "lite" version of the treat you gave up. In this example, maybe you could bring in a dessert from your favorite bakery, or give yourself a break from cooking and have pizza delivered, and drink a bottle of inexpensive Chardonnay. Or, you could cook dinner at home and go out to the movies afterward, if that's the part you miss the most.

Do give yourself some kind of treat, though, or you'll end up going on a bender, which could mean a whole *weekend* of dinners and fine wine. And think carefully about what part of your sacrifice you miss the most. Is it the fine wine? Watching the movie in a big theater while eating candy and popcorn? Or is it getting the break from cooking? Zero in on what you need the most and give yourself a taste of it.

Arrange a get-together with friends for the dinner and a movie night. Make it potluck to save money. Take turns hosting at each other's homes so it feels like you're getting out.

Track your progress. Have I ever mentioned my whiteboard addiction? Well, I have two huge whiteboards on the wall in my office. In fact, I used my whiteboards to help me organize the chapters for this book.

If you need a big reminder of how much debt is left— or, the glass half full version, how much debt you've paid off—then use a whiteboard for a weekly or monthly countdown. For example:

Week of March 29, 2015:

- Total credit card debt: $16, 294.55

- Amount paid off: $4,522.43

- Percent paid off: 28%

- Amount to go: $11,772.12

- Payoff target month: March 2016

You can change the numbers every week and watch the "Percent paid off" number get higher and higher. Sometimes a percentage sounds less daunting than an actual number.

You can see an example of a debt milestones worksheet here. In the blank worksheet you can figure out your target dates for 25%, 50%, 75%, and 100% debt-free milestones. Each milestone is worth an inexpensive celebration, even if it's just an $8 manicure.

MY DEBT MILESTONES

Starting Debt	$4,000	On Date:	7/1/2015
Milestone	Debt Paid	Debt Left	Reached On
25%	$1,000	$3,000	8/1/2015
50%	$1,000	$2,000	9/1/2015
75%	$1,000	$1,000	10/1/2015
100%	$1,000	$ --	11/1/2015

Along the same lines, you can monitor your credit scores. If you're using a free credit score website, you can track the number you're given. It's not a FICO score, of course, but it's still a starting point for a score, and watching that number go up will be gratifying. You can make a note of your FICO score, too, and when you decide to get an update on it, you can log in the number.

As you pay down your debt, your score will start to increase because your credit-utilization ratio will go down. This assumes, of course, that you aren't adding to your debt. Rule number one, people: No credit card spending until you're out of debt! This table also assumes that you're paying all of your other bills on time. Be diligent about this and your credit scores will improve.

Mind mapping. This technique is mainly used for business, but I think the potential for helping folks reach personal goals is untapped. For Visual learners, this approach is right on the money. Mind maps help you see the connection between what you're sacrificing now and what you'll get later on if you do. Mind maps can be as complex or as homespun as you like. There is software you can buy if you want to get fancy, but for our purposes, I think keeping it simple is best. I use a whiteboard for mine.

Start with a circle that shows your end goal. In your case, it's "Free From Credit Card Debt" or "Debt-Free." Put the circle in the center of your map and then branch out from there with key decisions and how they lead to your goals. You can also put the circle on the side of the paper or board and branch out in only one direction. For example, from the Debt-Free circle, you might branch out to saving for down payment on a house. From there, you branch out to sticking with your budget to save the money. It can really help to see your goal written down in black and white, and how today's sacrifices can help you get what you want tomorrow.

You feel doubtful

This is common when you're in debt. You're doing something really big here. You stared down your debt and now you're paying it off. That takes courage. But this is difficult, isn't it? It's normal to feel doubtful at times and wonder if you can even pull it off. Here is one of my best solutions that has always worked for me:

Have a theme song. Don't laugh; this is actually very effective. I had a theme song before it ever showed up on *Ally McBeal.* If you don't remember that show, it became famous for the dancing baby scene as well as the theme song of the main character. Ally was flighty and quirky and, of course, had a flighty and quirky therapist who recommended she get a theme song. Ally's theme song was *Tell Him* by The Exciters.

I've actually had a few theme songs over the years, but the one that gets me upbeat and makes me feel like I can climb a mountain is AC/DC's "Hells Bells." Maybe it's because I enjoy sports and that song shows up a lot in the NFL and the MLB. When I hear that song I'm ready to roll. When I'm going to do a TV interview, I play this song in my head. My brain recognizes it as a trigger that it's time to be "on" and to raise my game to a new level.

It's no accident that professional athletes have theme songs. The pros have known for a long time that this can be really effective when you need to kick things up a notch. Think about it: MLB hitters have a walk-up song when it's their turn to bat, and MLB closers always have a theme song that announces their arrival in the game. When an athlete hears his song, it signals his brain to be alert and to perform at a high level. When you do this repeatedly and you experience success, you develop a positive association between the song and your confidence to perform the task at hand.

Theme songs are good for performance when it comes to your job, but songs also can help you overcome a tough task in your personal life. When I was paying off debt, I often listened to *Man in Motion* by John Parr. I added this song to my MP3 player this past summer when I was writing this book. It helped me remember the ups and downs and how fired up this song got me. (Obviously you might have to change some lyrics to fit your situation—or gender!)

If you think about it, you've probably been drawn to certain songs when you've been going through a rough patch. We're all different, and different songs will speak to us and help get us fired up. I'll bet some of you would pick classical music or maybe even country. Here are some suggestions:

- "I Will Survive" by Gloria Gaynor
- "Thunderstruck" by AC/DC
- "Enter Sandman" by Metallica
- "Eye of the Tiger" by Survivor
- "Don't Stop Believin'" by Journey
- "Roar" by Katie Perry
- "We Are the Champions" by Queen
- "Don't Stop Me Now" by Queen
- "Light 'Em Up" by Fallout Boy
- "Counting Stars" by OneRepublic
- "Get Lucky" by Daft Punk
- "Party Rock Anthem" by LMFAO
- "How I Feel" by FloRida
- "Happy" by Pharrell Williams

Seriously, I could go on and on. Pick a song or two that really gets you psyched up when you're feeling low or just when you want to add some extra giddy-up to your stride.

You feel defeated

This doesn't mean you want to give up. It just means that facing your debt and making the uphill climb to get rid of it is hard to do. This might be temporary feeling because you've had a bad week or it might be more difficult to get rid of. Here are some suggestions that might help.

Have a girls' or guys' night out. I'm all for family togetherness, but it's okay to focus on yourself now and then and escape the family setting for a bit. This lets you take a breather from your routine, and when you're on a tight budget, your routine can start to feel like a noose around your neck.

Signs that you need a break from your loved ones: you're snapping at your kids or spouse over little things; you go on a tirade because the trash wasn't taken out; you feel as though your head will explode if you have to come up with *one more new way* of cooking chicken thighs. If this sounds like you, do yourself and your whole family a favor and get out of the house for a night.

Talk with a therapist. I've already mentioned that I was in therapy for years during my debt payback time. But I never mentioned to my therapist the fact that I was in debt. Well, I sure wish I had. There were times when I felt pretty down and out and needed some direction.

If you're feeling defeated, talking to a counselor might help. One of my readers talked to a credit counselor when he couldn't take it anymore. He and his wife were more than $60,000 in debt and were barely able to pay their bills. As it turned out, they received enough tips during their phone call to forge ahead on their own. You don't have to commit to three years of therapy to feel better about your debt. Sometimes one session—or just a couple of sessions—can help you clear your head and go forward with renewed optimism. But if you're struggling with depression over this, consider a regular weekly or biweekly session to help you get through this. I know it's expensive, so do some research and try to find a clinic that operates on a sliding pay scale. It doesn't hurt to ask a therapist if he'll consider doing that for you. And don't rule out health insurance. You might only be responsible for a co-pay, depending on what your insurance covers.

You feel alone

This is a bad, bad feeling. If you're single and in debt, you're probably going to feel pretty lonely at some point. It's hard to go through a crisis and not have someone there to commiserate with. Following are some suggestions to help you cope when you feel as though you're the only person in the world with credit card debt.

Find a debt buddy. This might be a friend who's in the same boat. Or it can be a friend who has zero debt but is supportive. Think about your social network and talk to someone who's upbeat all the time. You don't want a downer for a debt buddy.

Participate in a forum. There are amazing personal finance blogs and major Websites that have forums.

Get engaged with folks who are commenting. You can be anonymous on many of these if you like. I'm kind of private when it comes to money. I know that sounds insane because I've given you so much personal information. I'm private when it comes to how much money I make, but I'm very open when it comes to discussing mistakes I've made with money because I feel that can help others avoid the same fate.

If you feel comfortable chatting with others on a forum about debt, then you can benefit in a few ways. You can get tips and advice from others who are going through the same thing. You can also find much-needed camaraderie. I wish the Internet had been available when I was going through my debt disaster. I would have felt much less alone and less like a loser. When you're in debt, you think you're the only person to ever screw up with your money.

When you talk to others who are in the same debt trap, you realize it can happen to anyone—smart people, happy people, successful people. Just feeling normal again helps you stay on track with your debt escape plan. It really does help!

You feel as though you need a vacation

You have no idea how much I can relate to this. Whenever I'm stressed about anything, I dream of being on the beach under a big umbrella and sipping a mai tai. My number one escape from reality is the beach. Sometimes, just thinking about it helps; sometimes it doesn't help at all!

One way I cope when I need to get away, but can't, is to keep a Pinterest board titled "Places I'd like to go." I have way too many pins of Italy on this board along with photos of beaches I want to visit. Just keeping these photos acts like a goals list for me. I'm saving my money to travel to some of these places. I also have a "Places I've been" board; I like to look at these when I'm stressed out.

The best way to cope other than keeping your dream alive on a Pinterest board is to take a mini vacation. If you like the mountains, maybe you and your family can get away to a cabin for the weekend. A getaway to a bed and breakfast is also a fairly affordable way to take a little vacation and get away from home. Another option is taking a "staycation"—sleeping in, watching movies, giving yourself and your significant other spa treatments. This can be fun, too!

If you really can't afford to take any kind of break, whether at home or away, then make reservations on your calendar after your target debt-free date. You're debt-free in July? Plan a trip for August. This can really keep you motivated to stay on track.

You feel as though you've let your kids down

There was a time during the Great Recession when we cut back during the holidays. My husband and I are both self-employed, and we keep an eye on the economy. A few years back we were concerned and we had a smaller Christmas just in case our businesses took a dive. Plus, our daughter was starting college, so there was another big expense.

It was tough telling our kids that things would be tighter this year. But we knew it was temporary and we stressed that to them. We also promised to make it up to them the next year if our businesses were in good shape. So I understand that it's tough to look your 7-year-old in the eye and tell him that the holidays or his birthday aren't going to be what he's used to. But focus on the future and emphasize that it's temporary. Buy a lot of smaller, less-expensive items. I hate to say this, but volume can make up for a lot—affordable volume, that is!

You feel tension in your body

If you're in any kind of discomfort or pain, you need to see a doctor and make sure it's nothing serious. Once you're cleared by a medical professional, then try some of the tips that follow. Many of us get muscle tension when we're under stress. I was under a tight deadline when I was writing this book. I wrote for hours and hours a day sitting hunched over at my desk. Well, you know what happened? I ended up with a pinched nerve in my neck. I was in so much pain that I literally couldn't think straight. I couldn't even turn my head to the right. I looked like Frankenstein's bride.

I went to the doctor to confirm the diagnosis. I don't recommend playing around when it comes to physical pain. Don't ask your Facebook friends for their opinions and don't research your symptoms online. Unfortunately, I broke my own rule about Googling symptoms. By the time I got to the doc's office, my search results had me convinced I either had a brain tumor or meningitis. Naturally, this only increased my muscle tension.

I had inflamed neck and shoulder muscles that were in spasms. All of this led to a pinched nerve that radiated pain down my arm. I remember having something similar when I was in debt payoff mode. It got particularly bad when I was worried about my job security. How much stress can a person take, right?

So if you've been checked by a doc and you think your symptoms are stress-related, here are some things to try.

Take a walk outside. It's truly amazing how being in and around nature can help you relax. This can help you relieve stress because you're exercising. It also takes you out of your own stressed-out orbit for awhile. When I'm really uptight, I'll turn my walk into a "sensory walk." The results of this approach will vary based on the season, but here's an example of what I mean:

- **Sight.** Think about what you see on your walk. Look at the architecture of the homes and buildings that you pass by, look at the sky and notice cloud formations (not if you're on a busy street, though!), and look closely at any wild flowers or living creatures you come across.

- **Sound.** Listen to the birds, cicadas, or crickets, sirens in the distance, or laughter of children playing nearby.

- **Feel.** Think about how the wind feels on your skin, or how cold the water bottle is in your hands, or how glowing warm the sun is on your face.

- **Smell.** Notice the scent of freshly cut grass, the aroma of flowers, or the scent of rain.

Do some yoga. I've been doing yoga for years. Just basic stuff. I'm not a former gymnast, and I can't do the amazing backbends or balancing poses that many longtime, dedicated practitioners do. I just do simple yoga poses because it stretches my muscles and keeps me relaxed. You know how I mentioned the stress-related pinched nerve I got while writing this book? I felt so pressed for time that I stopped doing yoga. Big mistake.

You can do yoga by looking at poses or watching yoga videos online (free), taking a class at the local Y (inexpensive), or taking a class at a health club (more expensive, but it should be included as part of your gym membership).

Exercise or engage in sports. Sense a theme here? Working out, whether it's mild or strenuous, can help you fight muscle tension. Take an aerobics or dance class, play tennis, jog on a treadmill, lift free weights, play on a softball team, go horseback riding, or swim laps. Again, you have to be medically cleared to do a sport or engage in exercise, but if you can, exercise will help you cope. I wouldn't have survived without my four-times-a-week aerobics classes when I was in debt. It really kept me sane.

Scream into a pillow. This is an oldie but a goodie. And it's free. Let it all out; as long as you scream into a pillow, no one will call the cops.

Take a mental health day. If you can, take a whole day off from work and just relax. Sometimes you just need a break from life. Go to a movie during the day and eat popcorn. Take a walk by a river or lake. Take your dog for a walk. If you can't get an actual day off with pay, then wait until the weekend and go off by yourself or with the whole family. Get online and look for free or affordable events in your area.

You feel like you own the world

Cue your theme song! Champagne for everyone! Believe it or not, this will happen. You'll have days when you feel great because you're making progress. You're the debt ninja. Nothing will hold you back. You're confident and you know you can make it to the end and get out of debt.

But don't get upset when the highs are followed by lows. Remember: this is the emotional roller coaster known as debt. Just keep your arms and legs inside the car at all times, and you'll make it to the end of the ride in one piece.

***

The next chapter is for those of you who are experiencing a true debt disaster. For example, perhaps you can't meet your monthly obligations or you feel you're headed into bankruptcy. If you feel like you have your plan and you're on a steady, upward path, however, feel free to skip ahead to Chapter 9, where you'll learn about quick fixes for your credit score.

8

What If You're in a True Debt Disaster?

Credit card debt just by itself is stressful, to be sure. But there's a category on a different level that I call a true *debt disaster*. For instance, what if you lost your job during your debt-payoff process and now you can't make your minimum payments? What if your credit card accounts are so overdue they've all been sent to a collection agency? Or maybe you have more than $100,000 of credit card debt and there's no way you can meet the minimum payments; and, because your debt is so huge, the compound interest is making it worse every day.

If you identify with any of these scenarios, you're most likely at a point where you feel you're not only drowning, but going down for the last time. This is a scary spot to be in. When you're in way over your head, you might worry that it isn't even possible to pay off your debt without going into a debt-management program or even declaring bankruptcy.

Duct Tape Dilemmas

I think duct tape is one of the world's greatest inventions. It seems like it can be used for a quick fix for just about anything. Sometimes you can weather a temporary money crisis with a financial version of duct tape. These are solutions that help you just enough to pull you back from the brink of disaster—you know, those times when you can't pay your bills and you wish you were anyone else but you at the moment. If it's a short-term problem, there's a solution that just might help you survive it.

Check out the credit card hardship department

This is one of the best-kept secrets in the credit industry. This isn't a solution for someone who can't pay her bills and sees no relief in sight. These programs are designed for those who are in a temporary financial crisis. An example? You lost your job and it will be a few months before your new job starts. Or maybe you just got a divorce and your ex racked up some debt on your joint account.

What kind of relief can you expect? For six months to a year, you might get a lower interest rate or have your late fees waved. During this time frame you have to be diligent about sticking to your end of the bargain. If you pay late, the program could end. Also keep in mind that there's a good chance you'll have to agree to close your credit card account.

Here are four steps you need to take to inquire about your creditor's hardship program:

Step 1: The first thing to do is to write down a few bullet points describing your situation. If you've been an awesome customer up to this point, make that your first bullet point. The point of writing this out is so you sound in control of your situation when you are on Step 2, which is a phone call to your issuer.

If you sound flustered—or worse, panicky—it sends a message to the issuer that you're not really sure you're going to survive your financial crisis intact. Writing out the key points ahead of time will help you stay calm while discussing your dilemma. This is not the time to improvise and hope for the best. Here are a few things to keep in mind while you work on your talking points:

You must be honest about your situation, but don't go too far with the details. The last thing you need is to have the issuer feel uncomfortable with what you've said and decide to slash your credit limit.

Explain why you need temporary relief, and make it clear that you want to pay your bills.

Do you have a minimum payment in mind that you know you can pay every month? Explain that you've analyzed your budget and that's the amount you can handle until your situation improves.

Let the issuer know when you expect things to be back to normal. And keep in mind that hardship programs usually don't go beyond a year, so if you think your situation can't resolved that quickly, then this might not be the best way for you to proceed.

Step 2: Call your credit card company and ask for the hardship department. This isn't advertised, so it's possible you'll get a customer service rep who is uninformed. If this happens, hang up and call back 10 minutes later. Rinse and repeat until you get to someone who can help you. If the rep says that he isn't authorized to help you, ask for a supervisor. Keep going up the ladder until you find someone with decision-making power.

Step 3: Once you get the right person on the phone, you're ready to use your talking points. Explain your situation and then ask for a temporarily lower minimum payment. The catch is that you'll pay more in interest expense because you're extending the payoff period. So you can also ask for a lower interest rate to keep the interest expense in check. Keep a cool head no matter what the response. If you don't get what you need, try a gentle negotiation. Be polite and turn on the charm. If you aren't charming—and after all, not all of us have that ability—just be polite. Polite works, too.

Credit card companies vary when it comes to these programs, so there isn't a magic phrase that will work all the time. But it's amazing how far you can go in this life just by being a nice person and (politely) asking for what you need.

Step 4: Clarify what will be reported to the major credit bureaus. I already mentioned that you might be required to close your account, and this could ding your score a little. But it might help if the issuer reports it as "closed by consumer" instead of closed by the issuer. You also want to confirm that the issuer will report that you've made payments in the program as agreed.

Your score will rebound over time, but you have to be patient. This is not the time to obsess about it. Just know that closing an account on your own will look better to potential lenders in the future.

Get credit counseling sessions

Don't freak out. I'm not suggesting you leap into a debt-management program (DMP). Credit counseling can be an end in itself. But it is a resource you need to consider if you've been turned down for a hardship program and you're in dire straits. Hopefully you'll be able to access some information that can at least steer you in the right direction.

I've recommended credit counseling to a lot of my readers. Every week I receive e-mails from people who can't pay their bills. I'm so happy I can help and send them to a reputable counselor. There's only so much I can do, and I know when it's time to send someone to counseling.

For instance, if I hear from someone who has $54,000 in credit card debt and who can't pay his mortgage, then that's when I suggest he get professional help. Or if I hear from someone who has $10,000 in debt but can't stop spending, I recommend credit counseling for that person, too. In some cases, they only need a one-hour phone call to get turned around and headed in a more positive direction. Others, though, need full-blown counseling, help setting up a budget, and advice about what to do next. Some even need to go into a DMP, but those are in the minority.

A few things to keep in mind if you explore this option: **Choose a certified credit counselor.** You'll want to work with a member of the National Foundation for Credit Counseling (NFCC). Go to its Website, *www.nfcc.org*, and click on "Find an NFCC Member Agency." Agencies provide counseling on the phone, in person, and even over the Internet. The agency should be accredited by an organization such as the Council on Accreditation (COA). Being a 501(c)(3) nonprofit is also a good sign. There are for-profit agencies that aren't scams, of course, but if it were me, I'd work with a nonprofit.

You also should check with the Better Business Bureau (BBB) and your state's attorney general just to confirm that the agency you're considering hasn't had any complaints filed against it.

Prepare for the initial call. In many cases, you get a free one-hour phone call with a certified credit counselor. Use your time wisely by having your credit card statements, household budget information, and other debt information organized and ready.

Make a list of questions, too. If the counselor feels that you need further counseling to determine whether you need to consider a DMP, find out what the next steps are and what fees are involved. Any counselor that hesitates to discuss fees is not the right one for you. You only want to work with an agency that offers transparency and spends time thoroughly reviewing your financial records.

It's possible that the call will get you going on your own without any further need of help. I have a friend who had the one-hour call, took the advice, and managed to get out of debt on his own. He refinanced his car loan, set up a better budget, and stopped taking vacations until the debt was paid off. If you're thinking that he could have done that on his own—well, it's not that easy. Sometimes it's nice to have an objective person look at your situation. It takes the emotion out of it and suddenly the view is clearer.

Remember that credit counseling doesn't lower your credit score. I want to be clear about this because it's a common misconception that counseling negatively affects your score. The simple act of getting credit counseling will not trash your score. But if you connect with a company that expects you to stop make payments before an agreement is worked out, your score will definitely suffer if those missed payments are reported to the bureaus.

The Rules of Debt Collection

The Fair Debt Collection Practices Act (FDCPA) prohibits debt collectors from using deceptive, abusive, or unfair practices in their efforts to collect your debt. This law is enforced by the Federal Trade Commission (FTC) and the CFPB. The FDCPA covers personal, family, and household debts, including credit card debt. It does not cover business-incurred debt, however.

As defined by the FDCPA, a debt collector is an individual who regularly collects debts that are owed to others. A debt collector could be a lawyer or someone who works for a collection agency. There are also companies that buy delinquent debts and then try to collect those debts. Whoever they are, they can be overbearing. I remember a few collectors that really made me mad, but I didn't know my rights at the time, so I wasn't sure what, if anything, I could do about it.

Let's go over your rights so you can protect yourself from debt collectors that overstep the legal boundaries (or that just make you want to slam down the phone).

- **Time and place rules:** You can't be contacted at odd hours. A debt collector can't call you before 8 a.m. or after 9 p.m. And you can't be contacted at work if you've told them you aren't allowed to get calls there. You have to tell the collector this in writing or over the phone, though.

- **Privacy rules:** Debt collectors can ask others for your phone number and address, but they can't discuss your debt with anyone other than you, your spouse, or your lawyer. I was surprised to learn that they *can* ask others about your place of employment.

- **Information about the debt:** The collector has to send you a written validation notice within five days after they first contact you. This notice tells you the following: the name of the creditor to whom you owe the money, how much money you owe, and how to proceed if you believe you *don't* owe the money. They also can't communicate with you via a postcard. That wouldn't be very private, would it? I think talking about debt is a good thing, but that doesn't mean I want my postal carrier or my neighbors (if they receive my mail by mistake) to know my personal business. Along those same lines, collectors can't use an envelope that indicates they are in the debt-collection business.

Stopping the phone calls. If you write to the collector and state that you don't want any more phone calls, they are supposed to cease communications. There are a few exceptions to this rule, such as if the collector is attempting to notify you that they are planning a specific remedy. Send the letter by certified mail, but be sure you keep a copy of the letter. Remember: this doesn't mean the matter is resolved. You still owe the debt, but at least you won't have to deal with the calls.

How to respond: If you have the money to pay, consider talking to the collector. However, *proceed with caution*. Do not give your bank account information over the phone. It's not unusual to get pressured into giving a credit card account number or checking account number under the guise of resolving the issue immediately. The best way to proceed is to use your bank's bill pay service to pay the debt.

Responding to legal action. If you are sued by the debt collector, you'll need to respond—or get an attorney who will respond to the lawsuit—by the date specified in the court papers. Not responding opens up another can of worms, including the possibility that the debt collector will win a default judgment against you. The court might even award additional fees against you for attorney's fees or collection costs. Don't hesitate to consult with an attorney in your state so you can preserve your rights. State laws differ when it comes to the rules about what creditors can do. As you can see, trying to navigate this on your own isn't a good idea.

What debt collectors aren't allowed to do

If a debt collector does any of these things, he or she is breaking the law:

- They can't harass you, which includes threats of violence, obscene language, or threats to expose you to the public.

- They can't lie about your debt. For example, they can't claim you've committed a crime or misrepresent the amount you owe.

- They can't claim you'll be arrested if you don't pay.

- They can't say they'll garnish your wages unless they are permitted by law to do so.

- They can't give false credit information to the credit bureaus.

- They can't engage in unfair practices when they attempt to collect your debt. For example, they can't threaten to take your property (unless they really are legally able to do so), deposit a post-dated check, or try to collect unauthorized fees, interest, or other bogus charges.

If they violate the law, you can sue a collector in state or federal court. You must do so within one year from the date the law was violated. If this applies to your situation, contact an attorney for advice.

I could go on and on here, but I think you get the gist of it. If you're in this situation, I urge to go to the FTC's Website, *www.consumer.ftc.gov/articles/0149-debt-collection*, and get a thorough understanding of your rights. There's only so much I can include here, because this is just a small section of the book. Entire books have been written about this; one of the best, in my opinion, is *Debt Collection Answers*, by Talk Credit Radio host Gerri Detweiler.

Signs of a True Debt Disaster

Okay, let's say you're past the duct-tape stage. You believe there's no way to patch things together until you can pay off your debt. There's no shame in this. I want you to know that bad things happen to all of us. Even if you brought this on yourself by overspending or not paying attention to your finances, try not to beat yourself up. I do still hope you'll read this entire book, though, because you will be in a position to rebuild your credit in the future. It's important that you understand how you got to this point so you can avoid repeating the same mistake down the line.

All that matters now is making a decision and moving forward in a positive way toward a solution. Let's explore the beyond-the-duct-tape options you have.

Debt-management plans

If things are indeed that bad, a credit counseling agency might recommend that you pursue a debt-management plan (DMP). This is not a decision to be made lightly or without the input of a certified credit counselor who has reviewed your financial situation.

Here's how a DMP works. You deposit money every month with the credit counseling agency you've chosen to work with. The agency then uses your deposits to pay off your unsecured debts (for example, credit cards and medical debt). Your credit counselor also works with your creditors to possibly lower interest rates and fees and develop a payment schedule for you. How long does it take? It all depends on the circumstances. It could take four years or even longer. During this time, you usually have to agree that you won't apply for any other credit or use your credit cards.

However, because you pay the debt in full, this approach is better for your credit score than a debt settlement.

Debt-settlement plans

Credit-counseling agencies are usually nonprofit organizations, but companies that offer debt-settlement plans are usually for-profit companies. They are similar to DMPs in that they work on your behalf to negotiate terms with your creditors. But in this case the goal is to agree to a lump-sum settlement, which is less than what you owe. To raise the money for the payment, you may be asked to contribute monthly to a savings account.

Here are some major red flags that I see with these programs:

- They often counsel their clients to stop making payments to lenders. Yep, this is worrisome.

- If you stop making payments, your credit history is going to take a beating. While you're waiting for your settlement company to come to an agreement with your creditors, you're racking up fees, penalties, and perhaps even legal troubles.

- You might be asked to make these payments for quite a while before you reach a settlement. In the meantime, you're twisting in the wind with unpaid bills. This financial purgatory could go on for years.

- If you already can't pay your bills, it's unlikely that you'll get relief from this type of program. You could be trading one headache for an even bigger one.

Impact on your credit

It will show on your credit report that you paid less than the amount you owed. Unfortunately, potential lenders may see this as a sign that you don't pay as agreed. But even so, you want the settlement to appear on your report so it doesn't look as if you have a delinquent account that you never bothered to address.

I mentioned in the previous bullet points that settlements usually happen after you stop paying your bills for several months. That alone will damage your score. The late payments stay on your credit report for up to seven years. And even when you've paid, it will still show that you settled the debt.

Creditors may report that you are on a DMP, but they all have different credit reporting policies. Your certified counselor can answer any questions you have about this. If you don't pay as originally agreed on your DMP, the creditor could report that and that would impact your credit rating. And on top of all this, it's not free.

You've got to pay taxes on that

If you save more than $600 on your debt settlement, you'll owe taxes on the amount that's forgiven. For tax purposes, your forgiven debt is considered income. For example, if you owe $12,000 and your debt settlement calls for you to pay only $7,000, then you have to pay taxes on the difference, or $5,000.

There's a way out of this if you're insolvent, which means your debts exceed the fair market value of all of your assets. If you're insolvent, though, you have bigger problems than your tax bill. You should receive IRS Form 1099-C from your lender, but even if you don't, you're still responsible for filling out the form and reporting it on your tax return.

Keep in mind that there are some exemptions when it comes to cancelled debts, and the laws in your state might differ from federal laws. This is complicated, isn't it? Honestly, if you're in this situation, you should speak to a tax attorney and get professional tax help so everything is done properly.

Be aware of scams

There are many scams out there just waiting to take advantage of folks who are desperate for financial relief, whether it's from a DMP or a debt settlement program. Let me tell you right off the bat that if a company says they "guarantee to make your unsecured debt go away," it's a scam. And be wary if they ask you to disclose your personal financial information, such as credit card account numbers and balances, before they will give you information about the services they provide.

According to the FTC, here are more signs of a debt-elimination scam you should be on the lookout for:

- You're told you have to pay a fee before any services are performed.

- You're told there's a new government program to help folks get out of personal credit card debt.

- You're told to stop paying your debts or stop communicating with your creditors, but the company doesn't tell you about the serious consequences of doing so.

- They tell you they can stop those annoying debt collection calls and even prevent lawsuits.

- They suggest—no, they *guarantee!*—that your credit card debt can be paid off inexpensively, maybe even for pennies on the dollar.

- They tell you that you need to enroll in a debt-relief program *before* they review your financial situation.

- They insist you make payments into a DMP before they have your creditors on board with the plan.

Here's one more very important thing to keep in mind when you're trying to determine if a company is legit: Companies that are serious about helping you will want to educate you about personal finance before they take you down the DMP path. They'll want to make sure you develop money-management skills so you can stay out of debt in the future. In other words, a scam company is in it for a quick buck and couldn't care less about your financial future.

Bankruptcy Options

I've noticed some folks have a bit of a high-and-mighty attitude when it comes to bankruptcy. They see it as a moral failure. I am not one of those people. Who the heck am I to judge anyone else? Of course, most of us would prefer to pay our debts, but there are circumstances in which people feel they have no other way out. Bankruptcy is hardly an easy escape from debt. It takes a while to rebuild your life and your credit history after going through a bankruptcy.

I'm not a bankruptcy expert—legal or otherwise—so I can't advise you about whether or not this is your best option. I'm only going to give you the cold, hard facts and then point you in the direction of some excellent resources. If you're considering bankruptcy, then this section might help you gather enough information so you can decide what your next steps are.

Declaring bankruptcy isn't the free lunch some people seem to think it is. There are consequences, for sure. A bankruptcy stays on your credit report for seven to 10 years, depending on the type of bankruptcy you pursue. Take comfort in knowing that the impact on your credit score decreases as the years go by, so it won't be a black mark on your record forever. Still, it can have a negative impact during the early years as you rebuild your life. During this time it might be difficult to get new credit, for example.

There are two main types of bankruptcy: Chapter 7 and Chapter 13. The word "chapter" refers to the chapter of the Bankruptcy Code, which is found in Title 11 of the United States Code. Note that Chapter 11 is actually available to individuals as well as businesses, but this is far less common and only a good idea for someone who has debts that exceed the limits on a Chapter 13 bankruptcy.

Bankruptcies cost several hundred dollars ($300–$400) and they must be filed in federal court. There are also attorney's fees that are added on top of the filing fees. You can get all the details at *www.uscourts.gov*, but here are some of the main differences between the two types.

Chapter 7 bankruptcy

This type of bankruptcy is often known as a "liquidation" bankruptcy. With a Chapter 7 filing, a bankruptcy trustee cancels many, if not all, of your debts. A Chapter 7 bankruptcy takes about six months or so to be completed and stays on your credit report for 10 years.

You will have to complete credit counseling with an approved agency. The U.S. Department of Justice maintains a list by state at *www.usdoj.gov/ust*; click on "Credit Counseling and Debtor Education" to see the list.

In a Chapter 7, you complete documents that basically lay out your entire financial life. You'll list your property, debts, creditors, monthly expenses, and so on. There are exemptions that are in place to protect certain types of assets, such as a 401(K) plan. Any assets that are not exempt can be seized by the trustee, sold, and distributed to creditors.

There are guidelines about eligibility. For example, you can't file a Chapter 7 bankruptcy if you've received a bankruptcy discharge in the last six to eight years. Also, you have to pass a *means test* to determine if you truly are in a category in which you can't pay your bills. In simple terms, it's the difference between your monthly expenses and your monthly income. This gives you your "disposable monthly income."

You will need to consult with an attorney to proceed, but if you'd like to do your own online means test to see where you stand, go to *www.legalconsumer.com/bankruptcy/ means-test*. This calculator was created by Albin Renauer, JD, author of Nolo.com's "How to File Chapter 7 Bankruptcy." If you don't pass the test, then you will have to file for a Chapter 13 bankruptcy.

Chapter 13 bankruptcy

Whereas filing for Chapter 7 bankruptcy is a fairly quick process, a Chapter 13 filing can drag on a long time. In fact, it can drag on for up to five years. With Chapter 13, however, you get to keep your property while paying either all or a portion of your debt. Those who are trying to stop a foreclosure so they can keep their home might file Chapter 13.

This type of bankruptcy is also called a *reorganization bankruptcy*. To qualify, you'll have to show that you can meet the financial obligations that are set for you to repay your debt. There's also a limit on the amount of debt. You can't have more than $1,149,525 in secured debt or more than $383,175 in unsecured debt.

You'll receive a repayment plan that describes the details of each debt and how much you'll pay of each. The plan is overseen by a bankruptcy trustee. I already mentioned that the payment plan can last up to five years. That's because it depends on how much you earn and how much you owe. The details are driven by your income, state and federal laws, marital status, and your specific assets.

With Chapter 13, you may be able to retain your credit cards if they have no balance and aren't included in the filing. If you choose to use them, keep the balances low and pay the bill(s) in full every month. A Chapter 13 bankruptcy stays on your credit report for seven years.

The rub is that the repayment plan must also pass what's called the *best interest of creditors* test. This means that debtors must pay their unsecured creditors at least what they would have had under a Chapter 7 bankruptcy. In many Chapter 7 cases, unsecured creditors receive nothing. Nada. So this test is usually met pretty easily. Another test is called the *best efforts* test. This usually means that you must use a specific portion of your disposable income to pay unsecured creditors. And finally, your repayment plan must be approved by the court before it can be finalized.

Secured versus unsecured debt

To be clear, secured debts are debts that are secured by collateral. So if you don't pay a secured debt, the creditor can obtain payment by taking the collateral and selling it. An example of a secured debt is a mortgage. The many ways in which secured debts are paid are too complex and filled with too much legalese for me to even make an attempt. But if you move forward, a bankruptcy attorney will help you understand your circumstances, rights, and obligations.

Unsecured debts aren't secured by collateral. An example of an unsecured debt is credit card debt; medical debt is another. Generally speaking, unsecured debts receive a certain percent of your disposable income, the amount of which is determined by a number of factors. Sometimes only a small portion of unsecured debts get paid in a Chapter 13 bankruptcy.

Medical Debt

Tell me if this sounds familiar: You had a major medical procedure done and you received a bill for $400. You believe that your insurance company hasn't finished paying their portion. So you set the bill aside and wait. And wait some more. Months later, you receive a letter from a debt collector and you realize that the insurance company isn't planning to pay any more of the bill. You owe the entire $400 and now the delinquent account is on your credit report and dragging down your FICO score.

Unfortunately, for some folks, the $400 is more like $14,000. Anyone who's had a serious illness or been in an accident could be left in a financial disaster. Medical bills are the leading cause of bankruptcy, according to a 2013 NerdWallet Health study. The study also showed that more than 20 percent of the population struggled with healthcare bills in 2013. That's one in five Americans. Wow, right?

In a Chapter 7 bankruptcy, medical debt is considered a non-priority, unsecured debt. For those with huge medical debts, a Chapter 7 bankruptcy will discharge most, if not all, of your medical debt. But as I mentioned previously, you have to qualify for a Chapter 7. In a Chapter 13 bankruptcy, medical debt, like other unsecured debts, will be included in your repayment plan. The amount you end up paying depends on many factors. The portion of the unsecured debts you aren't required to repay will be discharged.

According to the Association of Credit and Collection Professionals (ACA International), medical debt in 2013 surpassed debt issued by financial institutions as the biggest target of debt collection activity (source: "The Impact of Third-Party Debt Collection on the U.S. National and State Economies in 2013," prepared for the ACA International, July 2014: *www.acainternational.org/files.aspx?p=/images/21594/theimpactofthirdpartydebtcollectiononthenationalandstate economies2014.pdf*).

A CFPB study showed that those who had paid off delinquent medical bills still took big hits to their scores (source: "Data Point: Medical Debt and Credit Scores," Consumer Financial Protection Bureau, May 2014: *https://files.consumerfinance.gov/f/201405_cfpb_report_data-point_medical_debt_credit_scores.pdf*). These accounts remain on your credit report and that's why it's been included in the score calculation.

Medical debt and your FICO score

The CFPB also concluded that paid-off debts were being over-penalized by the score and that this could even result in 16 to 22 points taken off your score (source: NerdWallet Health Finds Medical Bankruptcy Accounts for Majority of Personal Bankruptcies," NerdWallet.com, March 26, 2014: *www.nerdwallet.com/blog/health/2014/03/26/medical-bankruptcty/*). To put this in context, if you have a 700 FICO score, which is good, your medical debt could pull you down to 678, which is now a fair credit score.

Enter FICO Score 9, which is the latest model of the FICO score. According to FICO, the new score won't include collection agency accounts if they are paid off, even if they remain on your credit report. It doesn't matter if they're paid in full or settled. FICO Score 9 will also be able to tell the difference between medical debt and other types of unpaid debt.

So if a lender uses FICO Score 9 to calculate your credit score and you've paid off some medical debts, then your FICO score will be higher than it would be with an older model. Unfortunately, a lender can choose which FICO score to use, so there's no guarantee a lender will actually use this model. Hopefully, FICO Score 9 will gain popularity; if you've been affected by medical debts, you'll see your score rise.

What to do about medical debt

My focus is on credit card debt, but I know many people have medical debt on their credit cards and that's why I've included it in this book. You're in a difficult situation, and I feel for you. Sometimes, using multiple strategies is the best way to survive medical debt. If bankruptcy is not in the picture—and for your sake, I hope it isn't—take a look at these suggestions to help you deal with your debt:

- **Negotiate with your medical providers.** There are many parts to a medical bill. There's the possibility of lab tests, anesthesia, X-rays, and so on. Try to tackle each area separately and see if you can negotiate to reduce the cost. Tell the provider what you've been through, and how you're working hard to pay the bills but you need a break.

- **Talk to a credit counselor.** I know this keeps rearing its head, but if your bills are high, a counselor working with an agency can negotiate on your behalf and help you pay the bills in a DMP. This isn't ideal, but it's an option to consider if you have horrific medical bills.

- **Ask about payment plans.** A friend of mine had breast cancer and reconstruction, and her costs were outrageously high. She negotiated a payment plan with a low monthly payment. She knew she'd be paying off the debt for decades to come, but the monthly expense was doable; she just considered it a fixed expense.

- **Look for mistakes.** Errors on medical bills do occur. Check every line item and if something seems outrageous, call and inquire about it. You might even see something on the bill that doesn't apply to your situation.

- **Debt collection calls.** If you get calls, don't ignore them because that leads to worse problems. I really suggest you talk with a credit counselor at this point. If your debts are so big they've gone to collections, then you would benefit from talking with a professional.

I think medical debt is the most stressful of all debt. You're dealing with an illness or an accident, and now you've got debt to deal with, too. It truly isn't fair. And these days, even with insurance, you can pay through the nose. Hang in there and know that this will not last forever.

Resources for Debt Disasters

- National Foundation for Credit Counseling: *www .nfcc.org*
- ClearPoint Credit Counseling Solutions: *www .clearpointcreditcounselingsolutions.org*
- Approved Credit Counseling and Debtor Education Course Providers: *http://www.uscourts.gov/ FederalCourts/Bankruptcy/BankruptcyResources/ ApprovedCreditAndDebtCounselors.aspx*
- Nolo.com (free legal information; not a substitute for a lawyer): *www.nolo.com/legal-encyclopedia/ bankruptcy*
- American Bankruptcy Institute: *http://bankruptcy resources.org/content/other-resources*

- National Association of Consumer Bankruptcy Attorneys: *www.nclc.org/for-consumers/for-consumers.html*
- National Senior Citizens Law Center: *www.nsclc.org*

9

7 Simple Strategies to Boost Your Credit Score

You've worked hard. Maybe you've paid off your debt, or maybe you're making such good progress that you can now turn some of your attention to getting your FICO score back on track.

The seven strategies I will be discussing start with the assumption that you will pay *all* of your bills on time. Not just your credit card bills, but every bill you're responsible for. That's the foundation for improving your score. So are you all in? Okay, let's fix your credit score!

Your Credit Score

When you apply for credit, the lender pulls your credit report from one of the three major credit bureaus: Equifax, TransUnion, or Experian. The bureaus keep track of information that's reported about your payment history.

Your credit report also shows how long you've had credit, the number of accounts you have, and the type of accounts you have, such as revolving (credit cards) and installment loans. Unfortunately, if you've had some negative experiences with credit, that might show up on your report, as well. Examples include late payments, collection accounts, or judgments against you.

A lender reviews your report, called a *hard inquiry*, and requests a credit score from the bureau.

You actually have several credit scores

So why do I keep referring to a FICO score? Because to do otherwise creates chaos. About 90 percent of lenders use a version of the FICO score, and yes, that means there is more than one FICO score, too. There are FICO scores that focus on one particular aspect of credit. For instance, there are industry-specific FICO scores such as mortgage scores and auto scores. There are several FICO score variations that just relate to credit cards. Estimates vary, but there appear to be dozens of versions of FICO scores.

Here are a few other scores: VantageScore (gaining traction as of this writing), Experian Plus Score, Equifax Beacon Score, and TransUnion TransRisk Score. There are free scores you can get online from Credit Karma, Credit.com, and Credit Sesame, just to name a few. The free scores you get on these sites aren't FICO scores; you usually get a VantageScore or TransUnion TransRisk Score. These scores often cause confusion because consumers mistakenly think they're looking at a FICO score. I often receive e-mails from readers who are excited by their great score. I hate it when I have to burst their bubble. Really, I do. I just want everyone to be happy.

Having said all this, though, I do think that free scores have a place in your credit life. Most of these sites will give you a "grade" by category. So you can get an idea of your overall credit health, but not your actual FICO score. Don't get caught up in the hard-sell tactics. As I mentioned in the previous chapter, you'll see suggestions to sign up for credit monitoring and things like that. I cover these Websites and how to use them effectively in more depth in my book *Confessions of a Credit Junkie*.

Here's what we're going to do to make credit scores manageable. I'm going to talk about FICO scores in the general sense because the scores used by credit card issuers are most often a version of a FICO score. Otherwise, you and I both might go insane trying to analyze a topic that changes with the wind. So, I want you to focus on the basic factors that are a part of FICO scores.

The five factors in your FICO score

Use this information as a guideline for which factors you need to pay attention to. What's confusing is that the weight of each factor can vary by each profile. This is why one person's experience may or may not be applicable to your specific credit profile.

By the way, if you'd like to learn more about credit and FICO scores, go to myFICO.com. It's a great resource, and you can buy your FICO standard score for $19.99. You can also get your FICO standard score based on your credit files from Equifax, TransUnion, or Experian.

1. Payment history: 35 percent. Your payment history includes your credit cards, mortgages, personal loans, installment loans, retail accounts, and finance company accounts. I started this chapter by telling you that you had to pay all of your bills on time. Now you know why. This factor makes up a whopping 35 percent of your score.

So what if you mess up and make a late payment on your credit card account? It won't doom you to FICO mediocrity, but the impact does depend on how late the payment was, how often it's happened, and how recently it happened.

If you have more serious issues, such as a foreclosure or a bankruptcy, try to stay calm. And again, as with late payments, the amount matters, too.

By the way, there's not much of a difference in the way the FICO score handles Chapter 7 and Chapter 13 bankruptcies. For both types, the filing date is used to determine how long it's been since the bankruptcy took place.

Here's the bottom line about major negative items on your credit report: The more time that passes, the less impact it will have on your score. So stay focused on all the other things you can do to improve your score and let time take care of the rest.

2. Amounts owed: 30 percent. Remember we talked about your credit-utilization ratio in Chapter 1? Your ratio is the amount of credit you've used compared to the total amount of credit you have available on your credit cards. Keeping your credit ratio under 30 percent is the gold standard. But guess what? If you want to maximize this part of your score, keep it under 10 percent. I know that can be tough, especially if you have a low credit limits, but it really does have an impact.

The reason this is a big deal is because if you appear to be maxing out your credit cards, it looks as though you're headed for financial trouble. You look desperate for credit. This increases your risk profile, so you get penalized by the score.

Other than your credit-utilization ratio, the FICO score considers the amount owed on specific types of accounts. For example, if you have an installment loan, such as for your car, the score looks at the original amount and how much of it you've paid down. Paying down installment loans shows you have the discipline to borrow money and pay it back. The score gods like this!

3. Length of credit history: 15 percent. This part of your score considers how long you've had credit accounts, which includes the age of the oldest account, the age of the newest account, and the average age of all of your accounts. Obviously, a longer credit history is good for your score. But even if you don't have a long history, you can still have a very good score if you work hard to do well in the other areas.

4. Types of credit used: 10 percent. Remember those mix tapes way back in the '80s and '90s? The art of the credit score is kind of like a mix tape. The score rewards you for being able to handle credit cards, installment loans, mortgages, and so on. This doesn't mean you need to go crazy and buy a car and a house to improve your score. You just need a good mix, such as credit cards and maybe a mortgage.

I know there are some finance gurus who say you should never have credit cards even if you use them responsibly. But you should know that folks with no credit cards are considered higher risk. This isn't good for your score. The decision of whether or not to use credit cards is a complex issue that is discussed in greater depth in other chapters.

5. New credit: 10 percent. This factor causes people a lot of angst. If you have too many inquiries in a short amount of time, it can ding your score quite a bit. Each inquiry takes anywhere from zero to five points off your score.

If you're new to credit, the impact of multiple inquiries and new accounts will be greater than if you have a longer history. It makes sense. If you have only a few recent accounts and you add a new one, the average age of your accounts gets even shorter. If you have many accounts you've used over the years, a new account has limited impact, if any.

The score does recognize when you're rate shopping for a mortgage or auto loan, so your score doesn't take a big hit from either of these types of inquiries. But it's a different story with credit cards. Each inquiry can cause you to lose points off your score. One inquiry is most likely fine, but several will add up quickly. The good news is that although inquiries stay on your credit report for two years, the FICO score only considers inquiries from the last 12 months.

Important note: Checking your own credit report does not affect your credit score. I repeat: You can check your credit reports as often as you wish without any fear of lowering your score.

Strategies to Fix Your Credit Score

Following are seven simple strategies to help give your credit score a boost.

Strategy #1: Fix errors on your credit reports.

When you're in rebuilding mode, all the rules go out the window. I recommend getting a copy of your free credit report at *www.annualcreditreport.com/index.action* regularly (for example, once every four months). By this I mean you should request a report from each of the major bureaus once every four months instead of all at once. This way you can monitor your credit over the course of a year. You are also entitled to a free report from each bureau every 12 months, so make sure you obtain the reports you have coming to you.

What are you looking for?

You're looking for any type of error. An error can drag down your score. For instance, imagine you find a late payment reported and you never, ever made a late payment. And you know this aspect of your credit history makes up 35 percent of your FICO score. See how an error can screw up your credit score?

And errors do happen. A recent Federal Trade Commission (FTC) study showed that 26 percent of the 1,001 participants had at least one significant error in at least one of their three credit reports (source: "Report to Congress Under Section 319 of the Fair and Accurate Credit Transactions Act of 2003," Federal Trade Commission, December 2012: *www.ftc.gov/sites/default/files/documents/reports/section-319-fair-and-accurate-credit-transactions-act-2003-fifth-interim-federal-trade-commission/130211factareport.pdf*). I'm not one to promote hysteria, so I also want you to know that only 5 percent of them had an error that actually changed their credit rating to a significant degree. But still, checking your score regularly is all part of your due diligence when it comes to boosting your score. And there's a chance you might get a boost from it, too.

Check your personal information, your credit card accounts, installment loans, mortgages, and so on. Check amounts for accuracy. Be aware that your credit card balances may differ a little from what you think you owe if you've made a payment that wasn't posted before the issuer reported your account to the bureaus. Also be aware that each bureau might have different information about you, so you need to look at the reports line by line—no shortcuts!

Here's a list of the information you need to verify:

- Personal information: name, address, social security number, etc.

- Negative information such as collection accounts, late payments, or any past due accounts.

- Public records, which includes bankruptcies, judgments, and liens.

- Credit accounts, which includes your credit cards, mortgage, car loans, and personal loans. Here you'll also see your credit limits and recent balances.

- Credit history requests, which will also include the purpose for each request.

- While you're at it, be on the lookout for signs of identity theft, which can also wreak havoc on your score if someone opens an account in your name and maxes out the credit card. If you see an account that you didn't open, then you need to take action.

What to do if you're a victim of identity theft

- Ask one of the three credit bureaus to place a fraud alert on your file. The bureau you notify is required to notify the other two bureaus. The alert is free and lasts for 90 days. With an alert in place, a potential lender has to verify your identity before approving an application for credit.

- Order all three of your credit reports. When you place a fraud alert on your file, you're entitled to free reports.

- Contact the business that reported the fake account, if you can.

- Create an identity theft report and submit it to the FTC. Print a copy of the report. This copy is now your Identity Theft Affidavit, and you'll need to take it with you when you file a report with the police. Go to this link to print a copy of the affidavit: *www.consumer.ftc.gov/articles/pdf-0094-identity-theft-affidavit.pdf.*

You can get more detailed information on the FTC Website: *www.consumer.ftc.gov/features/feature-0014-identity-theft.*

What to do if you find an error

You need to send a certified letter with a return receipt requested to the credit bureau involved. Be sure you include copies (not the originals) of any documents that support your case. If the credit bureau decides you aren't making a frivolous request (this happens when people try to scam the bureaus to improve their credit), they are required to investigate the error within 30 days. When the bureau investigates the item, they have to forward the documentation you provided to interested parties to demonstrate that the information is inaccurate.

If the investigation concludes that the information on your report is indeed an error, then the creditor involved has to notify all three credit bureaus so the information can be fixed or removed from your credit report. You'll also get a written report from the credit bureau that conducted the investigation as well as a free copy of the corrected report.

Fixing an error on your credit report won't always lead to an increase in your FICO score, but there's always a chance it might. And when you're boosting your score, you don't leave any stone unturned. You can get really helpful information about disputing errors on credit reports on the FTC Website: *www.consumer.ftc.gov*. If you have my *Confessions of a Credit Junkie* book, I cover this topic in more detail; there's even a sample dispute letter on page 43.

Strategy #2: Use credit cards responsibly.

If you follow a certain financial guru, you're probably ready to scream at me for saying this. But guess what? Unless you're a shopaholic who needs to stay away from credit cards, this is an effective strategy for giving your score a boost. If you've decided to forgo credit card use, I respect that. And if you still have credit card balances, don't try this strategy; it's for those who have paid off balances and are out of debt. You can check out the other six strategies in this chapter.

You may already have credit cards or you may be in a situation where you got totally cut off from credit. Don't worry: I'm going to address both situations. First, let's take a gander at why this is a good strategy (if you're not a credit junkie, that is).

How using credit cards responsibly build your score

It's not enough to have a credit card. You have to actually *use* it to affect your credit score. This shows that you can be trusted to buy something on credit and pay it back on time. And that's the game we're playing here. We're building your credit reputation and that's based on trust.

So for the moment, if you still have credit cards, use them for small, necessary purchases and pay the balance in full by the due date. Interestingly, you don't actually get rewarded for paying on time; you're *expected* to pay on time. It's like having a job where you're required to be there by 9 a.m. You don't get a bonus for being on time, but you might get reprimanded or even fired if you're often tardy. You'll learn more about how to manipulate credit card balances to your advantage in Strategy #3.

But what if your score is so low that you can't get a credit card?

Use secured credit cards

If you don't qualify for an unsecured card, then try a secured credit card. This is one of the best tools ever to rebuild your credit. Now, before we jump into secured cards, I want to give you a warning about unsecured credit cards that target the bad credit market.

Unsecured credit cards designed for bad credit can be tricky. Read the terms and conditions very carefully. There are often monthly maintenance fees, high annual fees, and more fees of a creative nature. If you feel you must have an unsecured card and I haven't reviewed it on my Website, send me a review request and I'll analyze it for you. I'm serious—I do this all the time.

If you're open to having a secured credit card you have better options. Here's how a secured credit card works: You make a deposit into a bank account and that "secures" the card for you. You receive a credit card in the mail that looks just like an unsecured card. As well, your security deposit stays in your account, so you're actually using a credit card and purchasing items on credit. Make sure you choose a card that reports to all three major credit bureaus or it won't help you build credit.

There are varying degrees of quality when it comes to secured cards. To help you choose the best card you can qualify for, I have a ranked list of the best and the worst secured credit cards on my Website. Currently, I have reviewed more than two dozen secured credit cards. Each secured card on the list is also linked to one of my neurotically thorough credit card reviews.

By the way, if you have a parent or spouse in the military, there are some truly excellent secured credit cards available to you. You'll find them at the top of my list.

Become an authorized user

This isn't as effective as having your own account, but there are benefits. As an authorized user you are added to an account owned by an individual who has great credit. Therein lies the key: great credit. Choose someone who is responsible and doesn't go on shopping sprees. But you also need to do your part and use the card responsibly.

As an authorized user, you are not legally liable for any credit card debt that ends up on this account. If the account owner suddenly defaults, you will not be legally responsible for the debt. On the other hand, if you spend recklessly, you can have a negative impact on the account owner's credit. So be diligent about your expenses.

Strategy #3: Keep an eye on your credit card balances.

We just went over how to boost your score by using credit cards responsibly. Now, we're going to take a look at how to monitor the balance and use it to your advantage.

You're probably sick of hearing about the credit-utilization ratio, so hopefully you get the gist of how important it is now. It's important to keep your overall credit-utilization ratio below 10 percent when you're trying to boost your score. It's also important to keep an eye on the balance of each individual card. That's right: It's possible to have a low ratio but still have one card with a high balance. The score takes a peek at the total amount of credit used *and* at the balances on each card, so you don't want any one card to get maxed out.

Let's go through a couple of different approaches that will help you become a credit card balance pro.

Consolidate your debt on one card. It should be clear by now that paying down your debt will improve your score. Often, a good way to pay off debt and save money on interest expense is to transfer your balances to a credit card with a 0% APR introductory offer.

When you do this, though, it can lower your score because you've got so much debt on one card. If you transferred $3,000 of credit card debt to a balance transfer card with a $10,000 credit limit, you're most likely okay as long as you don't close the credit card accounts that you transferred the debt from.

But a more common scenario is that you transfer $5,000 in debt to a card with a $6,000 limit. See the problem? That's an 83-percent utilization ratio on one card. Even so, it's sometimes best to take a short-term hit on your score if consolidating your debt saves you a bunch in interest expense.

So just be aware of the impact of a large balance on one card. And don't consolidate your debt if you're planning to apply for a mortgage or other type of loan in the next few months. **Make credit card payments twice a month.** One of the things that folks often find confusing are the differences between payment dates and reporting dates. You might pay your bill in full by the due date every month, but if you had a high balance that got reported to the bureaus before your payment was posted to your account, then your utilization ratio for the month will be higher than what you expected.

This is a common problem for those who use their cards to pay for everything. I use my cards quite a bit for the rewards and then pay my bill in full. My credit card limits are high, though, so it doesn't have a major impact on my score even if there are timing issues with my payment. But what if you don't have high limits?

There are a few terms you need to know to be successful with this strategy:

- **Billing period.** This isn't standard because you can change your due date these days to accommodate your cash flow. But the period consists of one month. For example, your billing period might be June 19 through July 18.

- **Closing date.** This is the cut-off date for posting your purchases and payments. In the billing period example above, the closing date is the 18th of the month.

- **Reporting date.** The issuer (using the same example) will report your balance, payments, and so on within a few days of the 18th. This information affects your credit score.

- **Due date.** In our example, your due date would be around the 15th of August. Your grace period is between the closing date, the 18th, and the due date, the 15th.

So if you make a payment on the 14th, your balance has already been reported to the bureaus and it does not include your recent payment. So this is how you can pay your bill in full every month and still have a high ratio.

You can make two payments in a month instead of just one. Let's say your closing date on your statement is the 23rd. In this case, the issuer probably reports your balance within a few days of the 23rd. The information that gets reported—your balance, limit, and so forth—is a snapshot on a given day, really. So the snapshot could be taken before your payment is applied to the balance.

Here's how to outsmart the system: Make an additional payment one to two weeks before your closing date. By doing this, your reported balance after the closing date on the 23rd will be lower. And this will give you a lower utilization ratio. The other positive for making two payments during the month is that interest is calculated on a daily basis. So you end up paying less interest. Win-win!

So there it is. You're now officially a master manipulator of the credit-utilization ratio game. Congratulations!

Strategy #4: Increase your credit limits.

This one makes a beeline right for your utilization ratio. Increase your overall limit, and you can decrease your ratio. A lower ratio often results in a higher FICO score. Simple enough, right?

But as with all things credit related, there are traps to watch out for. One of them is pretty big, too.

Keep your cool. When you call your credit card company to ask for an increase, tell them you're working on improving your score and that's why you'd like an increase. I've done this myself, and the customer rep was impressed I knew about utilization ratios. This lets the company know you're on top of your game. You know what you're doing.

What you don't want to do is come across as if you needed the extra credit to make ends meet. If you've been paying your bills on time and keeping a ratio below 30 percent, you probably won't have to worry about this particular issue. I mention this because I've heard of people shooting themselves in the foot by talking too much during a call to request a credit limit increase.

Here's the big trap. It's entirely possible to talk yourself into a credit limit *decrease*. I'm not kidding. I know consumers who had the misfortune of their credit limit increase request resulting in a lower limit and lower credit score. So that's a risk you assume when you make the request. That's why this strategy is best used by those who have a score that's trending upward.

Open a new credit card account. This one's controversial because it's usually not good idea to get a new credit card that you don't need. Well, there are a few exceptions.

If you're what I call a Power User, a cardholder who makes a profit from his or her credit cards and never carries a balance, then go ahead and open a new card if you're after a bonus or rewards. But if you're reading a chapter on how to boost your score, you're probably not setting the world on fire earning rewards at the moment.

Basically, when your credit is in a fixer-upper state, you shouldn't be opening up new accounts willy-nilly. Now, having said that, there is an exception. Remember I said you should be cautious about asking for an increase if your credit score isn't in an upward trend? Your other option is to open a new credit card account instead of asking for a higher credit limit on a current card you hold. This can be a second secured credit card.

There's a lot of confusion about how the FICO score "sees" a secured credit card, especially if the card is reported to the bureaus as secured. Let me put your mind at ease. The FICO score doesn't give a rat's behind if your secured credit card is reported as "secured" or "unsecured" to the credit bureaus. The score's algorithm picks it up as a revolving line of credit. As mentioned before, both your credit limit and your utilization ratio are considered in the calculation. But the FICO score doesn't take off points because you're using secured credit cards. The score really hates late payments and high utilization ratios, though, so no matter how many cards you have, use them responsibly and keep your balances low. If you fill up your newfound credit limit with reckless spending, you'll defeat the purpose of your new card.

How many credit cards should you have? Just enough and not too many. Don't open too many at a time because that will lower your score a little; it also makes you look desperate for credit, which is a big no-no when you're in rebuilding mode.

Just one more point: The score doesn't care if your card is reported as secured, but when potential lenders look at your report, they might care. I think it depends on the nature of your credit request. On the other hand, if your score is low, and a lender sees that you're using secured cards to improve your score and rebuild credit, well, I think that makes you look responsible.

At the end of the day, it is what it is. I know that sounds trite, but it really fits here. You're doing what you need to do to rebuild your credit, and there will be both positives and negatives along the way.

Strategy #5: Don't close old credit card accounts.

I'd estimate that I get at least a dozen questions a week asking me if closing a credit card account will increase the FICO score. That is a myth. Closing a credit card account does not improve your score; often, it decreases your score.

When you close a credit card account, you lose the available credit (credit limit) associated with that card. Remember our old friend the credit-utilization ratio? I'm sure you have the definition memorized by now, so you already know that if you decrease the amount of credit you have available, your credit-utilization ratio will go up. When your ratio goes up, your FICO score usually goes down. The exact impact on your score really can't be predicted because there are other factors involved, as well.

When you're trying to boost your score, why take a chance on losing points? I'm not saying you should never, ever close an account. But be judicious about it. Keep the account open unless the account has a huge annual fee or some other distasteful fee you refuse to pay.

Another question I often get is about losing the credit history associated with the account you want to close. I can put your mind at ease here, too. Closed accounts don't suddenly fall off your credit report. In fact, closed accounts can stay on your credit history for up to 10 years. Now, if you're closing an account you've had for 20 years, then might really hurt when it does drop off your report.

Strategy #6: Negotiate with your creditors.

In Strategy #4, I noted that you need to keep your cool when requesting a credit limit increase. If credit cards had a list of Ten Commandments, at the top would be this: *Thou shalt not spook thy creditors.* What do I mean that? Don't act like you need their help. You need to appear in charge of your life (pun intended). Your approach will depend on what, exactly, you're negotiating about. What we're talking about here is removing or revising information that's hurting your score. Keep in mind that negotiating tactics work best when you've been a very good customer in the past. It's possible to be in debt and still be making your credit card payments on time.

Be ready for your close-up. Before your call, jot down your talking points. Did you lose your job for a few months? Were you ill? Even rehearse a little bit. You want to be sure you sound intelligent and sincere. Rehearsing doesn't make you insincere; it gives you a chance to be successful with your request because you aren't rambling.

Try to get late payments removed from your credit report. If there's a late payment item on your report and you have a good reason for the lateness, trying to get it removed from your report is worth a shot. Remember: Payment history is 35 percent of your score. Late payments hurt you!

You've got your script ready, right? All you have to do is call and state your case. Stay calm and collected. If you encounter a customer service rep who seems hostile, ask to speak with a supervisor. If the rep resists this, thank the person for his/her time and hang up. Wait 10 minutes and call back and you'll get a different rep. Rinse and repeat until you get someone who you feel is giving you a fair shake.

What if the credit card company isn't convinced? Offer a show of good faith. Perhaps you can offer to make two payments a month for a few months to ensure them that you're paying down your balance. Or tell them you've set up payment reminders so this can't happen again.

You might be required to write a letter to state your case. No problem—you've got your talking points ready to go!

A note about getting a credit card debt reduced

Let's say you settle a $10,000 credit card debt with a creditor for $5,000. The creditor will stop hounding you for payment and that's all good. But the creditor will report the $5,000 discount as lost income to the IRS. The IRS then wants to get the tax money from you. This is not good.

There are different arrangements that are available, including payment plans (also called a workout arrangement), lump-sum payment, and forbearance programs.

Should you pay an account that's charged off?

If your account has been charged off, then the credit card company doesn't expect you to pay your debt. It may have been turned over to a collection agency. So before you do this, stop and think carefully. Paying off a charged-off debt can actually lower your score.

A collection account will stay on your credit report for seven years. If you pay the debt, the date gets reset to your payment date. Then the seven-year clock starts all over again from that date. Newer debt drags down your score more than older debt. See the cycle here? You thought you were going to boost your score, but instead you got a kick in the gut.

Many people have moral qualms about not paying a debt that they legitimately owe. I'm one of those people. So here's what you do: You offer to pay the debt in full if the creditor will remove the item from your credit report. *Get this agreement in writing.* I know many who have been burned by false promises from debt collectors. Don't let that happen to you. Get the promise in writing.

Strategy #7: Get a credit-building loan from a credit union.

If you can't get—or have sworn off—credit cards, consider getting a small loan to give your credit score a lift.

This gives you a chance to show that you can handle credit. Even if you never plan to use credit cards again, you still need to have a good credit score because it saves you money on life insurance, health insurance, mortgage rates, and more.

The way it works is similar to a secured credit card. With a credit-builder loan, you decide how much your loan will be, say $1,200, and you put $1,200 into an interest-bearing account at the credit union or bank that's giving you the loan. Your deposit basically secures the loan so the institution has minimum risk.

Then you take out a loan for $1,200 and make payments on it to the credit union or bank. In this example, you might make 12 separate $100 payments for a year. How does this boost your score? You get credit for on-time payments, which is 35 percent of your score. As a bonus, you also get credit for an installment loan, which enhances your "credit mix." The types of credit you have contributes 10 percent of your score.

If you don't have the cash, look for credit unions that offer *credit-enhancement loans*. With this arrangement, the bank loans you a small amount, such as $500, that's frozen in an account, and you make payments on it.

I focused on credit unions here because they frequently offer these loans and they are very consumer-friendly places. Interest rates on these loans will vary quite a bit, so it's important to shop around and compare. To see if there's one in your area that you can qualify for, check out Credit Unions Are a Smarter Choice at *www.asmarterchoice.org.*

Some traditional banks offer them, too, so ask yours if it offers these loans and what the terms are. Wherever you get the loan, confirm that the lender reports your history to all three major credit bureaus.

Closing Thoughts

Now that I've told you how to boost your score, I'm going to tell you not to obsess over it. If you're still paying off credit card debt, that's your number-one concern. If you're out of debt, you can certainly try these strategies, but be patient: Some of the tips in this chapter will give you a boost within a few months, but some, such as the credit-building loan or secured credit cards, might take a year.

So work toward a higher score, but don't let the score give you nightmares while you're rebuilding. Timely payments and low credit card balances will take care of your score over time.

10

Debt-Proof Your Future

Now that you're well on your way toward making progress on your debt, that makes this the perfect time to think about the future. And I'm talking about a debt-free future. It's important to start developing a debt-free mindset right now while you're still getting out of debt. The pain of credit card debt is still clear in your mind. You know you never want to feel that way ever again!

You're on your way to a better life. You're working hard and you don't want this time spent digging out of debt to be wasted. As you break free from debt, you want to make sure it stays that way. Here are a few things to keep in mind to help you have a debt-free future.

Don't Live Within Your Means: Live Well Below Them

Living within your means is a concept that gets tossed around a lot. I've got a problem with it because it implies you're doing okay as long as your expenses don't exceed your income. So even if you only have $5 left over at the end of the month, you're okay. You're living within your means, by definition. Nope, that doesn't cut it.

You need to live pretty far below your means so you can save money. And then save some more money. And invest your money. And have a happy and comfortable retirement. And provide your kids with an education. But most of all, living way below your means helps you build your emergency fund and contribute to your IRA or your 401(K), whichever is applicable to you.

One of my favorite personal finance books is *The Millionaire Next Door* by Thomas J. Stanley and William D. Danko. Now, I'll be the first to say it's not a scintillating read, but if you stick with it, you'll internalize the concept that you need to live below your means to accumulate any wealth.

Most of us don't have wealthy parents and aren't heirs to a hotel chain; we have to build financial independence on our own. That's why you need to embrace the concept of living below your means. That really is your gateway to financial freedom.

I was guilty of living way *above* my means when I got into credit card debt. It took a financial disaster for me to realize I had to stop spending more than I earned. I truly lived as if each day were my last. I'm fortunate I didn't have a serious illness or an extended period of unemployment to deal with at the time. I don't know what I would've done, but it would been beyond difficult to cope.

Many of you are still in credit card debt and this probably sounds like a dream to you. I've been there and I know it's a frustrating feeling. You're wondering if you'll ever get to the point at which you can stop worrying about your monthly bills and save for the future. You'll get there. Stick with your debt escape plan and you'll succeed.

Stick With Your Budget

You chose a way to budget and track your spending back in Chapter 6. Now you have to stick with it. I've seen too many folks give up their budgets after getting out of credit card debt. That's a huge mistake. Credit card debt is right around the corner when you stop tracking your spending.

When you get out of debt, kick it up another notch. You'll have more space in your brain because you aren't stressed about debt. If you chose a budget program that has a lot of cool features, start taking advantage of them. For instance, if there's a goals feature, set up goals for retirement or for your emergency fund. Or start analyzing your spending categories every week. You'd be surprised at how much fun that is. And make it a habit to do a state-of-the-month financial checkup and look at reports.

Even if you're doing the cash envelope method or a simple worksheet, you can spend more time analyzing your spending patterns and setting your own goals, as we discussed in Chapter 7. There's something about having goals that can really keep you going.

If you have children (or plan to have them), there's another good reason you want to stick with your budget. You want to equip them with this knowledge so they have a bright financial future.

Be a Role Model for Your Kids

I once wrote a story for *Good Housekeeping* about how to answer the tough questions that kids ask about money. Every expert I interviewed recommended being honest with your kids—well, honest up to a point. The degree of honesty depended on the age of your child, of course, but the overwhelming view was that sharing the family budget and talking about how much to spend on things, such as the family vacation, was a good thing.

One of the questions I am asked most often is about teens and credit cards. People want to know if teens should ever learn about credit cards. I know this is a bit controversial, but here's my answer.

Why you should teach teens about credit cards

No, I didn't say you should *give* teens credit cards; I said you should *teach* them about credit. I'll go a step further and say that even if you don't use credit cards, you should teach them about responsible credit card use. Here's why:

Your kids will be getting credit card offers when they go to college or, at the very least, when they graduate. Do you want this to be the first time they look at credit card information? Trust me, the lure of paying for pizza parties will pull them in if you haven't set a foundation of knowledge.

If you think you can simply tell them never to get a credit card, then you have seriously overestimated your power over them at this point in their lives.

If you don't educate them, they will get a card—or two, or three—and most likely end up in debt. Empower them with knowledge so they can protect themselves if they decide to go ahead and get a card.

Teenagers need the truth about how credit scores affect their lives. Feel free to disagree, but those are the facts. You save money on many things in life when you have an excellent credit score.

I don't suggest making your teen an authorized user while they're in high school. Instead, when they get their first job, start them off with a debit card that's linked to their own checking account. If you think they're responsible enough to be an authorized user or to get a student card (or secured card) when they're at college, that's fine. You don't need to ask anyone on TV or on the Internet if you should give your kid a credit card. You're the expert in this case. You're in the best position to know whether it's a good idea.

I feel strongly that it's our job as parents to make sure our kids can survive in the real world, financially as well as emotionally. So we need to equip them with knowledge so they can make educated choices. You don't ever want your kid to go through credit card debt. When I graduated from college, I got into serious debt because I didn't know what I was doing when it came to my finances. You know how it started? Every night, when I went home after work, I'd check my mailbox: There would be tons of credit card offers. I was told how special I was and how much I deserved those cards.

I was naïve and bought into the hype. A credit junkie was born! And being a junkie, I wanted to experience the adrenaline rush of getting a new credit card over and over again. I applied for several cards all within a few weeks. I ended up with seven credit cards and proceeded to max out all of them. That's how I ended up in credit card debt.

So even if you think credit cards are evil, explain how they work to your kids. You won't be there when they're 22 years old and they're sitting in their apartment, sorting through the mail. Make sure they know the dangers and, if they choose to get a credit card, that they know what responsible credit card use is.

Your Financial Emergency Kit

When my kids were younger they played a lot of sports. My daughter played soccer, danced, and was a competition cheerleader. My son played soccer, basketball, football, and travel baseball. I think I've seen just about everything when it comes to sports, from bruises to cuts to two broken legs. For the minor stuff, I always kept a first-aid kit in the car. A financial emergency kit is similar to the first-aid kit I kept in my car, except that a financial emergency kit can keep you covered for a major financial disaster as well as minor emergencies.

An emergency fund

Every emergency kit needs an emergency fund. I've already talked about the importance of having this kind of fund, but now I want to talk about how to keep building it. I'm going to sound a little bit like the Terrified Tightwad here, but I want you to have a comfortable safety net.

Once you're out of debt, you need to increase your emergency fund so that you have a six-to-nine-month safety net on hand. I know a lot of experts use the three-to-six-month rule, but I don't think that's enough. Life gets awful messy at times. And if you have kids, pets, and a home to maintain, well, you need to be sure you have a nice cushion in case life takes a scary turn.

I have an emergency fund that would cover my basic expenses for more than a year. This is a bit of overkill, but I have it because our income is unpredictable. We don't get a salary and have a 401(K). Well, I actually have two 401(K)s from previous corporate lives, but they're small. They would cover about two weeks in assisted living!

My emergency fund didn't appear magically overnight. It took time to build it up to this point. I'm in my 50s, so I've been at this a while. And I have a big emergency fund because of the circumstances of my life. For example, I have an older home, one kid in graduate school, with another that just started college, and we all drive older cars. My husband and I are self-employed, so our income is subject to changes in the economy or in our industries.

You have to look at your own personal situation and decide how much you need. But I do recommend at least three months' worth of expenses, preferably six. If you don't have an emergency fund, start one today even if you can only put $15 in it.

So how do you build this fund? A dime at a time.

1. Save your change. When I was paying off my debt, I had a red cut-glass jar in my kitchen that belonged to my grandmother. She survived the depression, so I figured it had good money karma. I put all the change I found in this jar. If I bought something with cash, and there was change left over, it went in the jar. When the jar was full, I'd roll the coins and deposit it in my account. That's right. I wasn't kidding about a dime at a time.

2. Open an online high-yield savings account. You're probably wondering where to keep the money, right? I promise you I no longer keep my emergency fund in my grandmother's red jar. Alas, the days of really high-interest savings accounts are gone, but the available options can still bring a few dollars your way. Online savings accounts aren't perfect, but I think they're a good solution for building your emergency fund. There's a wide variety of perks and features. In fact, I think you'll be surprised at the choices these days.

You can check out rates, which will range from .75% APY (annual percentage yield) to .95% APY at the moment on Money-Rates.com, NerdWallet, and Bankrate.com. Not great, but better than traditional savings accounts, which are around .01%.

Make sure you only use an account that's FDIC-insured. What does that mean? It means that it's an account that meets the requirements to be covered by the Federal Deposit Insurance Corporation (FDIC). To be FDIC-insured, the account has to be in a bank that participates in the FDIC program. A variety of accounts can be FDIC-insured, including savings, checking, certificates of deposit (aka CDs), and money market accounts.

If the bank fails, your money is safe if it's insured by the FDIC. The limit is $250,000 per bank. So when you reach $1 million, you can put $250,000 in four different banks and be insured. See? I have high hopes for you.

Here are a few banks with FDIC-insured savings accounts for you to consider. Remember that the percents given were accurate at the time of this writing and may have changed since publication.

- **Ally Bank:** You get .90% APY. There's no minimum deposit amount to open an account, there are no monthly maintenance fees, and you can deposit checks remotely.

- **GE Capital Bank:** You get .95% APY. There's no minimum deposit amount to open an account, there are no transaction fees, and you have multiple ways to access your money.

- **Barclays:** You get .90% APY. There's no minimum deposit amount to open an account, there are no monthly maintenance fees, and interest is compounded daily.

- **American Express Bank, FSB:** You get .80% APY. There's no minimum deposit amount to open an account, there are no monthly maintenance fees, and you can link your savings account to another bank account to make transfers.

- **Capital One 360:** You get .75% APY. There's no minimum deposit amount to open an account, there are no monthly maintenance fees, and you can access your account from your smart phone.

- **Discover:** You get .85% APY. There is a $500 minimum deposit required to open an account, but there are no monthly maintenance fees and no minimum balance.

3. **Take advantage of credit card rewards.** This is an option once you're out of debt. You won't get rich this way, but it's a legitimate source of money that can go into your emergency fund. If you have a credit card that offers a check when you redeem rewards, deposit that check into your emergency fund.

You can also consider a credit card that helps you more directly. Fidelity has some credit cards that funnel your rewards directly into the Fidelity account of your choice. With the Fidelity Investment Rewards Visa Signature Card, for instance, you earn 1.5 points for each $1 spent on the first $15,000 in purchases per year. After that, you get two points per $1 in purchases. For every 5,000 points, you can convert them into a $50 deposit into your chosen Fidelity account.

You can choose from a variety of accounts, including Fidelity Cash Management Account, a brokerage account, and an individual retirement account. If you are all about college expenses, then you can also choose to fund a Fidelity-managed 529 account.

You can use your card for everyday purchases or by charging recurring monthly expenses on your rewards card. But remember: This method is only for those who are out of debt and feeling confident about using credit cards responsibly.

4. Make sure you have a low-APR credit card. Again, once you're out of debt, this is a good thing to have in your financial emergency kit. You may already have this in your kit, and that's fine; just try not to use it until you're out of debt.

A credit card with a very low interest rate can come in handy for an emergency. During the 2013 holiday season, I had two giant holes in my kitchen and laundry room ceilings. It was bad enough to go through the holidays like this, but my daughter had graduated from college and we had planned a graduation party for her between Christmas and New Year's.

Our roof had suffered wind damage and it developed a few terrible leaks. I knew we had a major problem when my son woke me up at midnight to tell me that there was water all over the kitchen floor. The contractor had to cut holes in the ceiling to find the sources of the leaks.

If you've ever had water damage, you know how expensive this can get. Well, I don't mind telling you that I was petrified. I had no idea if insurance would cover the cost.

Well, insurance sort of came through. The bill was around $20,000. Scary, right? Insurance agreed to pay for

$14,000, but we had to cover the remaining $6,000, which isn't a paltry amount. I used my low-interest credit card (9%) from Bank of America because I wanted to float the total expense for a month or two rather than drain my fund. In an emergency, sometimes it's better to pay a little interest instead of leaving yourself financially vulnerable.

If I didn't have the money, I might have had to carry a balance for a year or more. And if I didn't have good credit, I never would have gotten such a low-interest card.

Listen, even if you've decided to forgo the use of credit cards, I recommend you have one low-interest card that you can keep on hand for emergencies. If nothing else, it also gives you a revolving credit line on your credit report. Use the card responsibly every few months for a small amount so the issuer doesn't close it from lack of use. This also helps you maintain a healthy score.

5. Pay attention to the details. Speaking of credit cards, once you're using them again you need to pay close attention to any communication you get from your issuers. Did your APR go up? Get on the phone and find out why.

Check your online accounts a few times a week. At the end of every month, do some financial housekeeping. Check all of your investments and assess how things are going. This is a book about getting out of debt and I don't have the room here to get into details about having an overall financial plan, but I want to mention it because you need to think about it.

I take a holistic approach to personal finance. It might not seem that way because I'm so specialized. I do think when you have an emergency, like credit card debt, you have to focus on it to get rid of it. But when you're out of debt, take a more global view of things. Pay attention to every facet of your money, and that requires some long-term thinking.

6. Long-term care insurance. No one wants to think about this, but if you're over 47, put this on your radar. Or if you have a parent who might need it, read on so you can suggest some resources for them to explore.

You may not need it, and you don't necessarily have to plan for it, but I want you know the basics. I have had personal experience (my mom) with how much health-care costs if you ever need long-term care. It's ugly, folks. Downright ugly. Medicaid is an option, of course, but you have to use up most of your financial resources before you can qualify. You could lose your nest egg at that point. Well, that's another entire book!

Even so, I'm not going to recommend this across the board because having it doesn't guarantee it will even cover your needs. But when you're in your mid-50s, you should at least check it out. By the time you get there, the whole industry could be different. AARP has some good information on this kind of insurance, so I suggest checking out their site when you're ready to explore it.

Policies cost less if you get them before you have a health crisis. That's always the way it is, isn't it? And the premiums tend to go up as you get older, which is a problem if your income is going down. Other than individual plans, there are options such as employee-sponsored plans, plans sponsored by organizations (for example, professional organizations), and plans that might qualify for state partnership programs. The point is, if you feel this is something you or your partner should check into, then explore all of your options, including checking with your employer.

I didn't mean to be a downer there, but we're talking about staying out of debt long term so I wanted to give this topic a little space. Now, back to our regularly-scheduled, happy programming!

Your Long-Term Financial Goals

We talked about short-term goals in Chapter 7 and how they can keep you motivated when you get into the debt doldrums. Now let's think about long-term goals, because they can keep you motivated to stick with your budget and stay debt-free for life.

You can use a lot of the same techniques we talked about in Chapter 7, such as mind mapping, making vision boards, or just making a simple list. I've even put goals on sticky notes as a temporary measure. I often get ideas out of nowhere, so I'm addicted to those colorful sticky notes for capturing the random goals that pop into my head. If they pass muster after I think about them, they go on my goals list, which is kept in a Word document. Nothing fancy. I've recently started using Evernote, too, and it's a fantastic tool for such things. Check it out at *https://evernote.com/*.

I want you to think about setting goals even if you've still got $14,000 worth of debt left to pay off. Long-term goals give you purpose, and, believe it or not, they keep you focused on managing your money in the best way you can. You'll find that you want to reach your goals if you do a good job articulating exactly what they are.

How to create goals

Do you have a major expense in your future, such as providing your kids with a college education? Have you had a lifelong dream of owning a fishing boat? Or would you like to pay off your mortgage before you're 40?

There are no right or wrong goals. If your goal is to have a pool in your backyard, that's fine. I'd suggest you look into how it would impact your home's value and weigh the cost against that, but I'd never throw cold water on your dream. (Yep, pun intended.)

Have you heard of SMART goals? This a method designed to help people set goals in a way that makes reaching them more likely. It's used often in business, but I think it's a great approach for financial goals, too. SMART is an acronym for the following:

- **S**pecific: You don't want to be general. You want a boat? What kind of boat? How much will you spend?

- **M**easurable: How will you measure your progress to the goal?

- **A**ssignable: If you won't be doing all the tasks to reach the goal, who else will be involved?

- **R**ealistic: Is it a goal you can actually achieve? For instance, I'd love to be Olympic-caliber figure skater, but I don't think I can pull this off now. Yes, that ship has sailed. But I can set a goal to be become pretty proficient at my local skating rink.

- Time-related: When will you achieve this goal?

You can use the SMART goals approach to set personal goals, too. And anyway, some goals are both financial and personal. The swimming pool you want costs a lot of money, but it's something you want for your personal enjoyment.

Specific and challenging goals

I want to talk a bit more about the "S" part of SMART goals. For years, I had trouble making my goals specific. And I want to add my personal touch to this and say that your goal should also be a little hard to reach.

No, I'm not trying to stress you out by suggesting you make your goals a little challenging. Research on goal-setting shows that people who set specific goals that are a little difficult to reach are more successful than those who set easy goals. Be realistic (that's the "R" in smart goals), but don't make it too easy. If you have $250 in your emergency fund, don't vow to have $5,000 by the end of year unless that really is a possibility.

How specific do you need to be? It will vary by goal, but here are a few examples of specific goals:

General: I'll have an emergency fund by the end of this year.

Specific: I'll have an emergency fund that covers two months' worth of expenses by August 2016.

General: I'll pay off some of my medical debt soon.

Specific: I'll pay off two of my four medical debts in the next 12 months.

General: I'll contribute to a retirement fund sometime this year.

Specific: Every year, I'll add at least 10 percent of my income to my IRA.

General: I'll have a down payment for a house in a few years.

Specific: I'll save $2,000 per year in an account set aside for purchasing a home in 2019.

General: I'll save for an exciting family vacation when my oldest graduates from high school in 2017.

Specific: I'll save $1,250 per year for the next two years for a family trip to the Bahamas.

General: I'll start an account for my daughter's college education.

Specific: I can't afford to pay for all of my daughter's college education, but I'm starting a 529 plan and she'll have $10,000 to put toward her college expenses when she graduates from high school.

See what I mean by specific? It really does make a difference.

***

Now, here are four more rules to keep in mind as you go about setting your goals:

1. Make a commitment to your goals. Sometimes I have a hard time picking a goal because I can be a bit of a commitment-phobe. I'm that way about my career, too.

I still do a bit of freelancing because writing is in my blood, but these days I'm more focused on my blog and on writing books. Years ago, when I spent all my time as a freelance finance journalist, I was always trying to squeak in stories about health. I actually published some very nice health stories for major glossy magazines, such as *Health* and *Better Homes and Gardens.*

I did this because I had a phobia about specializing and making a commitment to finance writing. Eventually I stopped writing health stories because it wasn't a good fit for me. I also happen to be a hypochondriac so health research was very bad for my mental health. I started developing the symptoms I wrote about!

Anyway, once I got over my commitment-phobia and worked hard to develop my expertise in finance, and credit in particular, I became successful. So I'm asking you to think carefully about the goals you choose so they actually do motivate you to stick with your financial plan.

Now, having said that, I recognize that life circumstances change, and sometimes you need to change your goals. You might get a divorce or decide to make a career change and go back to school. You might develop a passion for travel and decide you'd rather focus on that than on getting a sports car. Or maybe your son has decided to go to an out-of-state school and now you need a bigger college fund.

You're free to change your goals as your life and interests change. But my point is that you want to set goals that you feel passionate about at the time. If you change them at some point, it will be to something you're equally passionate about, right? So the motivating force of your goals will continue.

2. Prioritize your goals. This isn't talked about often enough. If you're way behind on building your emergency fund, don't put a European vacation ahead of it. That doesn't mean you can't take a cheaper vacation. If you live near a beach, then you can drive there for a long weekend. I do want you to have fun. You need it. But extravagance has to wait its turn.

Right now, my goal list includes a trip to Italy in three years. I also have "learn Italian" on my list, and hopefully I'll learn Italian before I get to go to Italy. But I have to give other things priority so that's why Italy is three or four years away. I have college expenses to deal with for the next three years, so it wouldn't makes sense to spend that kind of money on a trip right now.

This book is about getting rid of credit card debt, which is toxic debt. That kind of goal takes priority. Once you're out of debt and you have a healthy emergency fund, you'll have more flexibility when it comes to prioritizing your goals.

3. Set short-term goals. Long-term goals are fine, but you also want to include short-term goals to help you reach them. Maybe you decide that putting $1,500 in your emergency fund within the next 12 months is your goal.

Your long-term goal can be six months' worth of expenses, but for now, you can break the goal down into stages. That trip to Italy I just mentioned? I'm putting aside a little bit every month to save for it. So my short-term goal could be to save $50 per month in a "much-needed trip to Italy" account. Having short-term goals are great for making you feel as though you're making progress toward a goal that's far away. That's why they help you when you're working toward wiping out a sizeable credit card debt.

4. Focus on your successes. I was once told that I'm annoyingly optimistic. No, I'm lying—I've been told that *dozens* of times by people who can't stand perky people. The truth is, I have down days when I want to gripe about my life; I just don't do it publicly very often. I find that when I do, I plunge into a downward spiral of negativity. And let me tell you, nothing good comes from that. Pity parties are often overrated. They just make all the participants feel even more terrible than before.

I have problems just like everyone else. But I find that if I'm pleasant to be around, I have more friends who are also glass-half-full people. In an earlier chapter I mentioned the expression that says you become the average of the five people you spend the most time with. Motivational speaker Jim Rohn said that.

I'm in a business in which rejection is a way of life. I lost count of how many times my book *Confessions of a Credit Junkie* was rejected by publishers. When I was a freelance journalist and I wrote for magazines, I was rejected a lot. I had some big successes, but I also had major rejections that made me want to give it all up and work at Starbucks.

But somehow I managed to keep going. I have a positive mind-set, and that keeps me afloat during stressful times. Baseball is another profession where you have to have a positive mind-set. A player with a .300 batting average is considered a very good player. That means that 70 percent of the time, the player fails. But the player changes his mindset so that the 30-percent success rate (at a minimum) is the goal.

In closing, I just remind you that you're awesome and amazing. Don't focus on the bumps you experience while getting out of debt. Focus on the successes. It's okay to feel angry if your boss cuts your hours and it messes up your debt escape plan temporarily. But once you shake off the anger, get right back up on that horse and adjust your plan to reflect your new circumstances.

So stay focused on your successes. That will help keep you confident as you pay off your credit card debt and build a great financial life!

Appendix A:
Glossary of Key Terms

Affinity card. A credit card that's usually offered through a partnership between an organization, such as a university or a sports franchise, and a financial lending institution. The organization's logo appears on the card.

Algorithm. A complex set of calculations that analyzes a set of data to produce a credit score. (*See also* credit score; FICO score.)

Annual fee. A yearly fee that some credit card companies charge for the use of a credit card. The fee is usually billed to the consumer's credit card account. Annual fees range from $29 up to $500 or more for elite cards.

Annual percentage rate (APR). The actual yearly cost of borrowing money. The APR includes fees and any additional costs and is applied each month to the outstanding balance on a credit card.

Application fee. Some credit card issuers charge a fee to apply for a credit card. This is more common with credit cards that target those with bad credit.

Authorized user. Someone who has permission to make purchases on a credit card, but who isn't legally responsible for any debt on the credit card.

Automatic payment. An automatic payment can be set up to authorize regular withdrawals from a checking or deposit account to pay credit card bills or other expenses.

Available credit. The difference between the amount of outstanding charges on a credit card and the account holder's credit limit. For example, if you have a $2,000 credit limit and your outstanding charges are $300, then your available credit is $700.

Balance transfer. A balance transfer involves transferring credit card debt from one credit card account to a new credit card account, which usually has a 0% APR.

Balance-transfer fee. The fee charged for making a balance transfer. It's usually between 3% and 5% of the amount transferred.

Bankruptcy. When consumers can't pay their bills, they sometimes go through a legal process and declare bankruptcy. A bankruptcy has a negative effect on credit scores, but the impact decreases as time goes by. (*See also* Chapter 7, Chapter 11, and Chapter 13 bankruptcies.)

Billing cycle: The period of time between one billing statement to the next. It's usually a one-month period.

Billing statement: A written or electronic statement that lists all of the transactions (purchases, payments, and fees) within a specified billing cycle. This is also called a monthly statement or an e-statement.

Cardmember agreement. Sometimes referred to as the fine print, the card member agreement provides terms and conditions and other cost information about a credit card. It also discloses information about dispute resolution. It's considered a contract, but the credit card issuer can make changes as long as they meet the legal requirements for notification. (*See also* credit card agreement.)

Cash advance. A cash loan from a credit card via an ATM, a bank withdrawal, or "convenience" checks. This is an expensive way to get quick cash. The interest rates tend to be very high and the interest starts accruing immediately.

Cash-advance fee. When you get a cash advance on a credit card, you have to pay a transaction fee. This fee is usually between 3% and 5%.

Chapter 7 bankruptcy. A type of bankruptcy in which a consumer's debts (most of them, at least) are discharged.

Chapter 11 bankruptcy. The type of bankruptcy that usually applies to businesses. It allows a business to restructure its debts. An individual can also file Chapter 11 if he or she meets certain requirements.

Chapter 13 bankruptcy. The type of bankruptcy that allows a consumer's debts to be restructured, rather than completely discharged. Then the debt is repaid over three to five years, under bankruptcy court supervision.

Charge-off (n.). The balance on a credit card that the issuer believes is unlikely to be paid. When it's written off as bad debt, it's a charge-off.

Collection. An attempt by a collection agency or department to get a past-due debt paid.

Consumer credit file. An individual's record at a credit bureau record. Credit files might include a consumer's name, address, social security number, credit history, inquiries, collections, and public records such as bankruptcy filings. Consumer credit files can differ by agency.

Co-branded card. A credit card that's usually offered through a partnership between a retailer, such as an airline or department store, and a bank or financial lending institution.

Co-signer. An individual who signs an agreement to pay off a loan for another person in case of default. For example, a parent might co-sign on a credit card for his or her adult child. This can be risky for the co-signer because he or she is responsible for any debt on the credit card.

Credit bureaus. These companies are sometimes called credit reporting agencies. Bureaus gather information about your payment history, credit, debt, and other aspects of your credit life. When a credit score is calculated, they use the information in your credit file. The three major consumer credit bureaus are Equifax, TransUnion, and Experian.

Credit card. A plastic card that allows you to make a purchase at the point of sale. Your card's terms and conditions and any additional features will be outlined in your credit card agreement.

Credit Card Act of 2009. Also known as the Credit Card Accountability, Responsibility and Disclosure Act of 2009. The Act gave consumers many protections, including limiting when credit card interest rates can be increased on existing balances, requiring 45 days' advance notice of significant changes in credit card terms, and, if a grace period is offered, giving consumers at least 21 days to pay their monthly bills.

Credit card agreement: A document that outlines the terms and conditions for using your credit card. It is your contract with the credit card company.

Credit card issuer. The bank or financial institution that offers credit cards to consumers. For example, Chase and Capital One are issuers, but Visa and MasterCard are only payment networks, not credit card issuers. However, American Express and Discover are both issuers and payment processors. (*See also* payment network.)

Credit counseling agency. Employs credit counselors who will talk with you about your financial situation and discuss repayment options with you. If you agree to a debt-management plan, these companies often try to negotiate with your creditors to get lower rates and fees. They usually charge a fee for their services, but the initial phone call is usually free.

Credit history. A record of your behavior when it comes to borrowing and repaying debt. Your credit history is viewed by lenders when you borrow on your credit card. Also called a credit line.

Credit limit increase fee. Some credit cards, usually those for bad credit, might charge this fee if you're approved for an increase in your credit limit.

Credit report. A report that shows your history of debts, repayment behavior, available credit, and credit inquiries. This is sometimes referred to as your credit history. Lenders view your report when you apply for credit.

Credit score. There are many credit scores, but in general, they are three-digit numbers that reflect how well you handle credit. Scores are calculated using an algorithm that considers a variety of factors, including payment history, credit-utilization ratio, inquiries, types of credit you have, and the length of your credit history. Your score, usually a version of a FICO score, is used by lenders to help them make credit decisions and set rates.

Credit-utilization ratio. The comparison of the amount of credit used to the total amount of credit available. Also called the balance-to-limit ratio.

CVV. The card verification value, also called the security code. For American Express, the CVV is a four-digit number on the front of the card. For Visa, Master-Card, and Discover, the CVV is a three-digit number located on the back of the card.

Debt-to-income ratio. The percent of your income that goes toward paying your debt.

Default. If you don't pay your credit card bill by the due date, you're in default. Usually, though, you won't be considered in default until delinquent for more than one 30-day billing cycle. But the issuer can apply a high "penalty" APR if you make late payments.

Delinquent. If you don't make even your minimum payment, you're delinquent. An account is usually categorized as 30, 60, 90, or 120 days late.

Due date. Your credit card bill has a due date, and if you don't pay your bill by the due date, you could be charged a late fee. You could also accrue interest charges if you don't pay in full during the grace period. (*See also* grace period.)

EMV card. A credit card that meets the standard for chip-and-PIN cards that are used in Europe. EMV stands for Europe, MasterCard, and Visa. In the United States, chip-and-signature cards are becoming more common. Issuers are expected to offer chip-and-PIN cards at some time in the future.

Equal Credit Opportunity Act (ECOA). Federal legislation that prohibits discrimination in lending, including credit cards. Originally, ECOA was enacted in 1974 as Title VII of the Consumer Credit Protection Act.

Fair Credit Reporting Act (FCRA). Federal legislation that promotes the confidentiality, accuracy, and proper use of information in the files of the major credit bureaus. The FCRA was enacted in 1970. A 2003 amendment enabled consumers to get a free credit report from each bureau every 12 months.

FICO scores. Credit bureau risk scores that are produced from models developed by the **Fair Isaac Corporation (FICO)**. FICO scores are the credit scores used most often by lenders to assess credit risk when a consumer applies for credit. These scores are calculated based on the information available in credit bureau reports.

Finance charge. The amount of interest you pay when you carry a balance.

Fixed rate. An annual percentage rate (APR) that stays the same and doesn't move up or down with the prime rate.

Foreign transaction fee. Fees that are charged on purchases made in a foreign currency or on purchases that involve a foreign bank. These fees usually range from 1% to 3%, but there are some credit card companies that waive foreign transaction fees. CapitalOne and Discover don't charge them on any of their cards. There are other major issuers that waive these fees on specific cards.

Foreclosure. If you don't meet your loan obligations on your mortgage, a bank can threaten to foreclose. This is a legal proceeding in which the bank tries to recover the balance of the loan by taking possession of the home and selling it.

Garnishment. A court order that allows a debtor's wages or other income to be taken and paid directly to a creditor or court until a debt is paid in full.

Go-to rate. Interest rate, or APR, you are charged after your introductory rate ends.

Grace period. The time period in which you can pay your credit card bill in full and avoid paying interest charges. Grace periods are usually between 20 and 25 days long.

Hard inquiry: A credit inquiry from a potential lender that reviews the details of your credit report. A hard inquiry can lower your score. (*See also* soft inquiry.)

Hold. With credit cards and debit cards, a portion of your credit limit is put on "hold" if the final amount of your transaction is in unclear. For instance, this often happens at gas stations and hotels.

Inquiry. When you apply for credit, the lender looks at your credit report to decide if you should be approved. This action is called making an inquiry. A soft inquiry doesn't hurt your score, but a hard inquiry does.

Installment debt. Debt that is paid at regular times and over a specific period. For example, a car loan is installment debt.

Interest rate: The cost of borrowing money. With credit cards, the interest rate is usually stated as the APR, so it includes the cost of yearly fees.

Introductory APR: With some credit cards, you get an introductory APR when you open a new account. It lasts for a specified period of time and, when it ends, your new APR is the go-to rate. Introductory rates are sometimes called teaser rates.

Joint account. A credit card account that's owned by two or more people. The parties involved equally share legal liability for any debt.

Judgment. A court order to pay a specified amount to someone who filed a lawsuit against you.

Late payment fee. The fee that is charged when you make a delinquent payment (a payment that is received after the due date).

Minimum interest charge. The minimum amount of interest you will be charged, if you are charged any interest at all.

Minimum payment. The lowest amount of money you're allowed to pay in a given billing cycle, if you don't pay your entire balance.

Opt in. Giving your credit card company or bank permission to include you in a particular service.

Opt out. Declining a particular service or a change in the terms of your credit card contract.

Over-the-limit fee. A fee that's charged to your account if your balance exceeds your credit limit. You will not be charged this fee unless you have authorized opted in allow transactions that go over your credit limit.

Payday loan. A short-term loan that usually doesn't require a credit check. These loans are very expensive and should be avoided.

Payment network. A network of companies that handles credit card payments among merchants, credit card users, and credit card issuers. The four major ones are Visa, MasterCard, American Express (also an issuer), and Discover.

Penalty APR. The APR you'll be charged on new transactions if you do something that triggers the penalty terms. The terms vary by issuer, but it's usually paying late, exceeding your credit limit, or bouncing a check. These rates can be very high. If you're more than 60 days late, the penalty APR could be applied to your entire existing balance.

Piggybacking. Improving your credit score by becoming an authorized user on someone else's credit card. The account owner must have excellent credit for this to work.

Preapproved. If you're preapproved for a credit card, it means you pass the initial screening process. You still have to apply, and approval isn't guaranteed.

Premium credit card: These credit cards usually have high credit limits, rewards, and excellent benefits and perks.

Prime borrower. A prime borrower has an excellent credit history and gets the lowest rates from credit card issuers and other lenders.

Prime rate: The rate that banks charge their most creditworthy (or prime) customers (usually businesses). Credit card issuers use it as an index to set rates for their customers. Most APRs are variable, and they move up and down with the prime rate. APRs are prime plus a margin.

Purchase APR. The APR you pay for purchases if you carry a balance on your credit card. If a credit card doesn't have a grace period, this is the rate of interest you start paying when the transaction is posted to your account.

Re-aging. Re-aging a debt means the clock starts anew on the statute of limitations. This extends the time that a creditor may use the courts to collect that debt. For example, if you make a payment—or even a verbal commitment to pay—on a debt that has exceeded or is approaching the end of the statute of limitations, the debt may be re-aged.

Revolving credit. A line of credit that doesn't require a specific repayment schedule. Credit cards are revolving credit.

Revolving debt. Debt that you owe on a line of credit that doesn't require a specific repayment schedule. Credit cards are an example of revolving credit.

Schumer box. An actual box on the terms and conditions page that clearly discloses the rates and fees for a credit card.

Secured credit card. Secured cards help people with limited or bad credit establish or rebuild a credit history. A deposit is made into an account to "secure" the card. The security deposit usually equals the credit limit, though some cards allow a higher limit than the deposited amount.

Secured debt. Debt that is backed by collateral. For example, a mortgage is secured debt; if you don't pay as agreed, the lender can seize your property.

Soft inquiry. A credit inquiry that doesn't review the details of your credit report and has no impact on your score. Examples include checking your own credit report, business that check your credit for the purposes of offering you a product or credit, and companies who already have a relationship with you who check your report. (*See also* hard inquiry.)

Statute of limitations. The amount of time that a creditor or a debt collector has to sue you for unpaid debt. The time period varies by state and by type of debt. Be aware that a debt can be re-aged if you make a payment, or indicate that you will make such a payment, on a debt that is past the statute of limitations. (*See also* re-aging.)

Terms and conditions. Card issuers describe various practices in detail in this part of the disclosure statements. It's considered a legal contract.

Truth in Lending Act (TILA). The TILA is the primary federal law that governs the extension of consumer credit by lenders in the United States. Congress instituted the Act in 1968 to protect consumers against inaccurate and unfair credit billing and credit card practices. It requires disclosure of credit terms so that consumers can comparison shop for certain types of loans. A part of TILA is Regulation Z, which is administered by the Federal Reserve. Regulation Z offers more consumer protections, including requiring credit card issuers to disclose the terms and conditions to potential and existing cardholders at various times.

Universal default. Before the CARD Act, this was a common practice. Cardholders who failed to make timely payments to other lenders, such as mortgage lenders and car lenders, would see their APRs raised by the their credit card issuer, even if they paid their credit card bills on time.

Unsecured credit cards. Credit cards that are not secured by any type of collateral. For example, if you don't pay your bills, issuers can't take your property. This is why you need good credit to get an unsecured card.

Unsecured debt. Debt that isn't backed by collateral. Two examples are credit card debt and medical debt.

Variable-rate APR: An APR that goes up and down with the prime rate, unless another index, such as the LIBOR rate, is specified.

Zombie debt. Old credit card debt (and possibly other kinds of debt) that is past the statute of limitations, which means a debt collector can't use the courts to collect the debt. Sometimes collectors will still try to collect them, however. So these debts are like zombies. They keep coming back from the dead.

Appendix B:
Resources

Equifax Credit Information Services, Inc.

P.O. Box 740256

Atlanta, GA 30374

(800) 685–1111

www.equifax.com/home/en_us

TransUnion, LLC

P.O. Box 2000

Chester, PA 19022

(800) 888–4213

www.transunion.com

Experian

P.O. Box 9701

Allen, TX 75013

(888) 397–3742

www.experian.com

Information on Credit Scores

MyFICO.com: *www.myfico.com/SEO_Home.aspx*

Credit Bureaus and Credit Scoring: *www.usa.gov/topics/money/credit/credit-reports/bureaus-scoring.shtml*

VantageScore: *www.vantagescore.com*

General Consumer Information

Consumer Financial Protection Bureau (CFPB): *www.consumerfinance.gov*

To submit a credit card complaint to the CFPB: *https://help.consumerfinance.gov/app/creditcard/ask*

Federal Trade Commission, Credit and Loans: *www.consumer.ftc.gov/topics/credit-and-loans*

Federal Reserve Education Credit Resources: *www.federalreserveeducation.org/resources/topics/public_credit.cfm*

Better Business Bureau (BBB): *www.bbb.org*

Consumer Action: *www.consumer-action.org*

Contact Information for the Canadian Credit Bureaus

If you have dual citizenship in Canada and the United States, you cannot merge your credit files. You have to maintain separate credit files for each country.

Equifax Canada

Equifax Canada Co.

Box 190 Jean Talon Station

Montreal, Quebec H1S 2Z2

www.consumer.equifax.ca/home/en_ca

To order free report by phone: (800) 465–7166

To order free report by mail or fax use this request form: *www.equifax.com/ecm/canada/EFXCreditReportRequestForm.pdf*

Fax number: (514) 355–8502

Procedures to dispute an error: *www.consumer.equifax.ca/dispute-ca/dispute_process/en_ca*

Follow the instructions on the home page to order your Equifax Credit Score.

TransUnion Canada

For English correspondence:

Attention: Consumer Relations

P.O. Box 338, LCD1

Hamilton, ON L8L 7W2

8:00 a.m. to 8:00 p.m. ET (Monday to Friday) at (800) 663–9980

For French correspondence/En Françias:

Centre de relations au consommateur

CP 1433 Succ. St-Martin

Laval, QC H7V 3P7

8:30 a.m. to 5:00 p.m. ET (Monday to Thursday) and 8:30 a.m. to 4:30 p.m. ET (Friday) at (877) 713-3393 or (514) 335–0374 (in Montreal)

www.transunion.ca

Overspending problems

Debtors Anonymous: *www.debtorsanonymous.org*

Credit counseling

National Foundation for Credit Counseling: *www.nfcc.org*

*Note that all NFCC members are accredited by the council on Accreditation for Children and Family Services (COA), which is a not-for-profit independent accrediting body. The COA has accredited—or is in the process of accrediting—about 1,400 programs by the United States and Canada.

ClearPoint Credit Counseling Solutions (formerly CredAbility) is a member organization of the NFCC and accredited by COA: *www.clearpointcreditcounselingsolu tions.org*

Mortgage Information and Resources

U.S. Department of Housing and Urban Development: *http://portal.hud.gov/hudportal/HUD*

Books on Personal Finance

Note: I've listed the paperback or hardcover editions, but most of these are available as ebooks, too, which will save you some money.

One of my favorite authors, personal finance expert and columnist **Liz Weston**, has written several books you should check out:

- *The 10 Commandments of Money: Survive and Thrive in the New Economy* (Plume, 2011)

- *Your Credit Score: How to Improve the 3-Digit Number That Shapes Your Financial Future*, 4th Edition (FT Press, 2009)

- *Deal With Your Debt: Free Yourself from What You Owe*, Updated and Revised (FT Press, 2013)

Jean Chatzky, financial editor for the *Today Show*, is another personal finance rock star. I've read all of her books. You might find these particularly helpful:

- *Money Rules: The Simple Path to Lifelong Security* (Rodale Books, 2012)
- *The Difference: How Anyone Can Prosper in Even the Toughest Times* (Crown Business, 2010)
- *Pay It Down! Debt-Free on $10 a Day* (Portfolio Trade, 2009)
- *Money 911: Your Most Pressing Money Questions Answered, Your Money Emergencies Solved* (HarperBusiness, 2009)

Clark Howard is my consumer advocate role model. I'm not quite as frugal as he is, but I admire him for the bargains he finds and the way he protects consumers. He wrote these two books with Mark Meltzer and Theo Thimou:

- *Clark Howard's Living Large for the Long Haul: Consumer-Tested Ways to Overhaul Your Finances, Increase Your Savings, and Get Your Life Back on Track* (Avery Trade, 2013)
- *Clark Howard's Living Large in Lean Times: 250+ Ways to Buy Smarter, Spend Smarter, and Save Money* (Avery Trade, 2011)

Gerri Detweiler is a well-known and highly respected personal finance expert and the director of consumer education on Credit.com. She's also the host of *Talk Credit Radio*. If you have debt questions, you'll find great advice in her books. These books can be ordered on her Website: Gerridetweiler.com.

- *Debt Collection Answers: How to Use Debt Collection Laws to Protect Your Rights*, published by Credit.com, written with coauthor Mary Reed

- *Reduce Debt, Reduce Stress: Real Life Solutions for Solving Your Credit Problems*, coauthored with Marc Eisenson and Nancy Castleman (Good Advice Press, 2010)

Michelle Singletary is an award-winning syndicated columnist for the *Washington Post*; her columns are a must-read for me. Check out her latest book:

- *The 21-Day Financial Fast: Your Path to Financial Peace and Freedom* (Zondervan, 2014)

Farnoosh Torabi is a personal finance expert and TV personality. She's written some terrific books:

- *When She Makes More: 10 Rules for Breadwinning Women* (Hudson Street Press, 2014)

- *You're So Money: Live Rich, Even When You're Not* (Three Rivers Press, 2008)

- *Psych Yourself Rich: Get the Mindset and Discipline You Need to Build Your Financial Life* (FT Press, 2010)

Lynette Khalfani-Cox is another personal finance expert who has written terrific books. Check this one out: *Zero Debt: The Ultimate Guide to Financial Freedom, 2nd Edition* (Advantage World Press, 2008).

Some Classic Books I Recommend:

- *The Millionaire Next Door* by Thomas Stanley and William Danko (Gallery Books, 1998).

- *Think and Grow Rich* by Napoleon Hill (Wilder Publications, 2008). The original version was published in 1937 and there are many editions available on Amazon.

- *Your Money or Your Life: 9 Steps to Transforming Your Relationship With Money and Achieving Financial Independence: Revised and Updated for the 21st Century* by Vicki Robin, Joe Dominguez, and Monique Tilford (Penguin Books, 2008)

Ilyse Glink is a nationally recognized real estate expert. If you're thinking about a buying a home, I highly recommend these books:

- *100 Questions Every First-Time Home Buyer Should Ask: With Answers From Top Brokers From Around the Country* (Three Rivers Press, 2005)

- *Buy, Close, Move In! How to Navigate the New World of Real Estate—Safely and Profitably—and End Up With the Home of Your Dreams* (William Morrow, 2010)

Resources if You Have Student Debt

CliffsNotes Graduation Debt: How to Manage Student Loans and Live Your Life, 2nd Edition by Reyna Gobel (Cliffs Notes, April 2014).

FinAid, the SmartStudent Guide to Financial Aid

Student Loan Borrower Assistance: *www.studentloan borrowerassistance.org*

U.S. Department of Education's Federal Student Aid: *https://studentaid.ed.gov/repay-loans/disputes/prepare*

Index

C

About the Author

Beverly Harzog is a nationally recognized credit card expert, author, and consumer advocate. She's appeared on Fox News, FoxNewsLive.com, ABC News Now, NY1, CNN Newsource, and in major media markets, including New York City, Philadelphia, Boston, and San Francisco. She's also a frequent guest on syndicated radio shows across the country, including ABC News Radio, and is the consumer credit advisor for the popular Website LendingTree.com.

Her advice can also be found in print and on major Websites, including the *Wall Street Journal*, CNNMoney.com, the *New York Times, Kiplinger, USA Today, Money*, ABCNews.com, NBCNews.com, the *New York Daily News*, the *Washington Post*, Time.com, *Consumer Affairs*, Associated Press, *U.S. News & World Report*, TheStreet.com, Yahoo! Finance, MSNMoney.com, Reuters.com, Inc., *Entrepreneur, Family Circle, Real Simple, Black Enterprise*,

Bankrate.com, CNBC.com, the *Atlanta Journal-Constitution*, the *Chicago Tribune*, the *Boston Globe*, and more.

Harzog is the author of four books. Her last book, *Confessions of a Credit Junkie* (Career Press, 2013) was featured in or mentioned by hundreds of media outlets. It was chosen by the *Washington Post's* syndicated columnist Michelle Singletary as her December 2013 Color of Money Book Club pick. *Confessions of a Credit Junkie* also received an outstanding book award in the Self Help/Service category from the American Society of Journalists and Authors.

She's also the coauthor of *The Complete Idiot's Guide to Person-to-Person Lending* (Alpha Books/Penguin, April 2009) and *Simple Numbers, Straight Talk, Big Profits: Four Keys to Unlock Your Business Potential* (Greenleaf Publishing, June 2011).

She's a regular speaker at College Week Live, the world's largest online college fair, and at national conferences, including the American Society of Journalists and Authors and FinCon: Where Money and Media Meet.

Beverly is a former CPA and has an MBA from the University of New Haven in Connecticut. She also spent two years in a doctoral program at the University of Georgia studying speech communication. She lives with her husband, their two children, an emotionally needy Maltese named Marshall, and a water snake in Johns Creek, Georgia. She's an exercise junkie, loves to listen to music (everything but country), and is a lifelong Atlanta Braves fan.

Contact Beverly:

Follow her on Twitter: @BeverlyHarzog. Or, get the latest buzz on credit cards and paying off debt by visiting her popular credit card blog at *www.beverlyharzog.com*. She considers herself the piano player of credit card reviews and will write a review on any card by request.